HOW TO Ul

GW01464191

Dee Rimmer

*

How to
Unlock Your
Potential

A PRACTICAL WORKBOOK FOR PERSONAL
DEVELOPMENT

12 keys *to unlock the wonderful creative
power within you and transform your life!*

Published in 1992 by Dee Rimmer, 1 Darwin
Court, Gloucester Avenue, London NW1 7BG

Reprinted 1993, 1995

© Copyright Dee Rimmer 1992

ISBN 0-9518662-0-6

British Library cataloguing-in-publication
data applied for

Electronically composed in Century 11/12pt
by Scriptmate Editions

Manufacture coordinated in UK by
Book-in-Hand Ltd
20 Shepherds Hill, London N6 5AH

Dedication

This book is dedicated to all my students both past and present, from whom I have learned so much.

And to my husband Tom, whose wonderful support throughout the years has helped me achieve my dreams.

May we all continue to grow from strength to strength.

Contents

INTRODUCTION

This is a serious work book. It is a book of clear instruction on how to change your life by understanding yourself.

If you understand how you function as a human being you can then clearly understand why people and circumstances seem to be against you.

You will be able to control your own destiny.

You will no longer be at the mercy of people, situations or circumstances.

You will know how to use the great, creative power that is within yourself.

Every aspect of your life will change for the better. You will uncover talents and abilities that you do not realise you have. You will be healthier, happier, more prosperous and self-fulfilled than you could imagine.

Regard this book as a manual of self-instruction.

You will be working on yourself, learning about yourself and other people.

Regard it as a course in Personal Development and Growth. Like any other course of study there must be total commitment and dedication. If you just read through it then you will end up with so much accumulated knowledge and no real difference to your life.

If you work consistently as it is meant to be used, then miracles will happen in your life.

THIS IS THE WAY IT WORKS.

1. There are 12 keys and each key has 4 sections.

2. Each key is to be studied for one month.

3. All the exercises and suggestions MUST be carried out.

4. Do not read through the book first as though it is a novel. THIS IS MOST IMPORTANT.

Take it step by step as you would any other course of study.

5. Before reading the first key you will need the following:

A mirror, a photograph of yourself, white file cards and a black felt-tipped pen.

6. THIS IS PREPARATION. Collect all the items above. Also start a file for yourself.

Make your own notes of all the results you experience and any comments you feel guided to write at the time. All this will help you to firm things in your own mind. This is a serious study you are undertaking, so honour it and yourself by giving it your best shot.

YOU ARE BETTER THAN YOU THINK!

7. The journey of a thousand miles begins with the first step. Take that first step with total commitment and dedication and you will never look back.

Students constantly write to me about their successes and great success can be yours if you settle down and seriously apply what you learn.

8. NO ONE CAN DO IT FOR YOU. You are the only person who can change your life. I cannot do it for you. All I do is show you how. I help you to help yourself!

9. It makes no difference how well or how poorly educated you are. I was forced to leave school at 14 years of age. I never lost sight of my dream to make something of myself. When I was 35, married with three children, I had the urge to change my life. At 37 years of age Manchester University saw my potential and gave me a chance. I have never looked back.

10. Age, race, sex, colour or creed is no barrier to self improvement. In fact, you owe it to yourself to be the best you can possibly be.

This 12-step plan has been very carefully formulated to help you achieve whatever you want in life.

What is your need at this moment?

Do you need money, love, work, home, good personal relationships, peace of mind, job satisfaction?

Whatever it is this plan will help you achieve it.

The simple instructions are easy to follow, but you have to do more than just read them. YOU HAVE TO OBEY THEM!

There are two ways of learning.

FIRST, by reading, listening and observing. This is the intellectual way of learning, a gathering of knowledge.

SECOND, by experiencing. This is the true way of learning.

It is only by actually doing something that you learn it. For example, you can learn the theory of music, but until you start putting that theory into practice by playing a musical instrument, you are not really learning music.

KEEP A LIGHT TOUCH. Do not allow yourself to get bogged down or be too serious as you put the plan into action. This course should be enjoyed not laboured over. Try to regard it as an exciting adventure, because that is what it is. You are about to change your life and that is certainly exciting. In fact, it's GREAT!

If you feel there is something you have not understood, then you need to take it more slowly. Each section must be worked on slowly and with patience. Remember, Rome was not built in a day and you have all the time in the world.

This plan is designed to cover a period of 12 months with 4 lessons each month. There is a monthly question paper which should be answered. This is a simple way of assessing whether the subject matter has been understood, and also a way of consolidating what you have learned.

Read each key first as a whole, as you would read a book and without obeying the instructions or doing the exercises. Then take one lesson at a time and work on it for a week.

Do not hurry this. Your mind needs time to assimilate what you read and work on. So, slowly does it. Rushing through it and skipping bits will slow down your progress and you will not fully understand what you are doing.

Do the exercises in each section, but do not stop the exercise you are working on. That means you will be doing the first exercise during the second week as well as the new one, and during week 4 you will be doing all 4 exercises.

REPETITION IS ESSENTIAL!

Thousands of students have proved and are still proving the success of this plan which I formulated nearly thirty years ago. It helped me when I first started teaching and later when I became Headmistress of a secondary school.

I take regular workshops and seminars and lecture both here and in the U.S.A.

From an ordinary background, I was determined to make something of my life. Despite severe illness and seemingly impossible setbacks I never lost sight of my dream. I STAYED WITH IT! There were times when in sheer desperation, I felt like giving up. Then I would devise little things to do that would help me over the bad times when things seemed hopeless.

As you work through the lessons you will no doubt find ways in which you can help yourself stay on course. If you do, I shall always be pleased to hear about them.

If you can find someone to work with it will be a great help to you both as you can encourage each other and talk things over together.

DO NOT DISCUSS what you are doing with anyone unless you know them very well and they are interested in trying to improve themselves. Unless they are of a like mind they will not understand what you are doing and they will criticise and laugh in ignorance. This is not to condemn them. This is to show you they are not ready to improve themselves yet.

Their comments could upset you and make you waver in your resolve to have a better life. The change in you will begin to show and they will see for themselves.

Good luck, enjoy it, and if you work at it you will enjoy life as much as I do. You will have the personal success that you can only dream of now!

KEY 1. RECOGNITION.

SECTION 1. YOU ARE A V.I.P.

You are a V.I.P.!

You are a very important person.

You are a wonderful, unique, creative being, with talents and abilities you have yet to realise.

> *Do you realise the importance of*
> *the above statements?*

Read them over again.

Now read them out loud.

It does not matter if you feel a bit silly doing this or if you believe the statements or not.

> *These statements are TRUE about YOU!*

Now, let us put these statements into the first person and see how you feel about them.

I am a V.I.P.

I am a very, important person.

I am a wonderful, unique, creative being, with talents and abilities I have yet to realise.

Now, say these three statements out loud *three times.* GOOD!

If you have obeyed the instructions then you have made an excellent start on a course that will change your life—if you will let it.

If on the other hand, you have not obeyed the instruction, then you are simply not giving yourself a chance, and that is sad for you have great potential.

YOU HAVE THE POTENTIAL FOR GREATNESS.

What stops you from achieving greatness? YOU STOP YOURSELF!

You limit the great power within you by saying such things as

"I don't have any talents."

"I'm only ordinary."

"What's good enough for my parents is good enough for me."

"I'm too old."

"I'm never lucky."

"I'm not educated."

All these sayings came from past students when they first started the course. We soon changed all that!

Here is another little exercise which must be done now! Get a mirror or find a recent photograph of yourself. LOOK AT YOURSELF. Either look in the mirror or at the photograph. LOOK AT YOURSELF CAREFULLY. *The person you are looking at is totally unique.* There is no other person in the world who looks exactly like you. (even identical twins are different)

You are the only person in the world with that face. No other person in the world has your smile. No other person has your mind. Your fingerprints are uniquely yours. Your body cells are uniquely yours. Everything about you is *uniquely yours.*

No one else can ever be the same as you and you can never be the same as anyone else.

THIS POINT CANNOT BE

OVER-EMPHASISED.

You have your own unique talents. No one else can do things the way you do them so you have a tremendous contribution to make in this life.

YOUR TALENTS ARE NEEDED.

You are special. You are unique and that makes you very important!

The person you are looking at is totally unique. You are rare, one of a kind, like a Rembrandt or the Koh-i-noor diamond.

No other person can be like you, no other person can fill your place in the world.

YOU ARE NEEDED!

Look at yourself again and then repeat the V.I.P. statements.

"I am a V.I.P."

"I am a very, important person."

"I am a wonderful, unique, creative being, with talents and abilities I have yet to realise."

Write these three statements on a card—a white file card—and carry this card with you wherever you go during the day. It can be in your pocket, your bag, on the dashboard of your car, on your desk, in fact anywhere you can look at it without drawing attention to yourself.

It is important *NOT* to tell others what you are doing at the beginning. They will not understand and their ignorance will weaken your resolve to change your life. At the end of the course they will see the difference for themselves and will marvel at it. So, keep it to yourself! *SECRETS!*

Let's look in the mirror again or at the photograph. See the potential that is in the person you are looking at.

Get a notebook or a piece of paper and make a list of all the things you like about yourself.

FIRST the physical appearance, the *outer qualities,* e.g. nice eyes, smooth skin, beautiful hair, lovely teeth etc.

SECOND the inner qualities, the character traits, e.g. kindhearted, cheerful, honest, hardworking, reliable, enthusiastic, etc. Keep checking the mirror or photograph and remember you are listing all the *NICE things* about yourself. Be honest. You will be surprised at the things you write down as you keep looking at the mirror.

THIS LIST IS VERY IMPORTANT!

Whenever you feel a bit low or depressed take out the list and mirror. As you look at the reflection repeat out loud all the things you like about yourself from the list. This will be a real morale booster and at this stage you need all the help you can get.

Let's go back to the beginning again. Reread the whole section and obey the instructions. Do this every day especially first thing in the morning and last thing at night.

The instructions should be carried out for 21 consecutive days. If you miss a day then you start the next day at *DAY ONE*. By doing this you will be commencing a good, constructive habit which is the start of something *BIG*.

YOU CAN DO IT!

Go on, force yourself! You will find that after a while you will be doing it without thinking about it. When you first learned to drive you had to consciously make an effort to learn the gear changes, etc. You concentrated very carefully upon what you were doing. You made mistakes and felt frustrated at times. Well that is the learning process. Eventually you found that you were doing all the things automatically, learning to drive had become a habit. It was now locked into your subconscious mind and your SCM reacted and worked on it for you. Simple, isn't it?

Keep it lighthearted, make a game of it. It s fun! We laugh a lot in our classes when we do these exercises and the other ones to come. We can take ourselves too seriously you know. So lighten up, loosen your belt and have a go.

THINGS TO DO FOR THE WEEK.

1. Say out loud the three V.I.P. statements. Do this first thing in the morning and last thing at night.

2. Read these statements from your card at odd times during the day.

3. Look at the photograph or mirror and read your **nice list,** at least once a day and more often if you are depressed.

THE PERSON YOU ARE LOOKING AT IS A V.I.P.!

REMEMBER — SECRETS!

KEY 1. RECOGNITION.

SECTION 2. WHAT DO I THINK?

You can do almost anything you want to do!

You CAN do anything you THINK you can do!

You CAN'T do anything you THINK you CAN'T!

You can if you think you can; you can't if you think you can't. What you think about yourself becomes a reality in your life.

Deep down within us all is an inner picture or blueprint of ourselves and this inner picture determines what we become in life.

How did this picture get there? From the day you were born you were bombarded with statements, beliefs and prejudices of everyone around you in your environment. You had no choice in this, all you could do was accept these opinions which were expressed about you.

If you displeased an adult you were smacked or harsh words were sharply spoken to you. You were not always aware that you had displeased the adult but you felt hurt and upset by the words that were spoken. Remarks were made that were totally untrue but you did not have the critical faculty necessary to screen them out. If an adult said, "You can't do that," you were not to know that the statement meant "you can't do it at this moment in time because I do not have the time to deal with it right now." You simply took it to mean that you did not have the ability to do it. Teachers and other people would also say similar things and it began to dawn on you that you did not have much ability.

This thought pattern would be firmly established in your memory bank and it became part of your blueprint. Throughout your life that one thought pattern could stop you achieving anything worthwhile.

When it comes to tackling something new how do you react to the challenge? Are you immediately enthusiastic about it and do you tackle it with great interest? Maybe you would love to do it but something seeks to stop you and you say things that are really excuses for not trying.

It is the thought pattern of failure that is embedded deep in your mind that holds you back.

YOU CAN CHANGE ALL THAT! If your thoughts are successful, happy thoughts then you will be successful and happy. If your thoughts are depressing failure thoughts then you will be a depressed failure.

IT'S AS SIMPLE AS THAT!

Try this exercise. Close your eyes for a moment and think about an unhappy event in your life. How do you feel?

Now think about a very happy event in your life. How do you feel?

The feelings you get whilst thinking about these two events in your life should prove what we said about our thoughts. There is a decided difference between the two thoughts.

YOU HAVE FREEDOM OF CHOICE! This is an important point to remember. You can change your thoughts anytime you want to change them. The emphasis is on personal choice.

You are the only thinker in your world. NO ONE CAN THINK FOR YOU.

Other people can tell you what they think and they usually expect you to think the same way as they do. What others think is alright for them, but you think your own thoughts and your thoughts are important for you.

When you express your thoughts you are giving your opinion about something. Your opinion has been reached by drawing your own conclusions from the evidence at your disposal and this is coloured by your memories.

WE ARE ALL AT DIFFERENT LEVELS OF DEVELOPMENT. Our development is our consciousness, our awareness, our beliefs at any given time and this constantly changes as we grow and develop.

From the day we are born we go through a constantly

changing pattern of development. If you look back 5 years you will see how you have changed in every aspect of your life. Go back further. In fact it is a good exercise to make a time plan of your life from the day you were born.

TIME LINE. Draw a horizontal line as long as you wish on a fair sized piece of paper. Put your date of birth at the beginning of the line and your present age at the end of the line. Mark off on your line every seven years of your life leaving a small gap between each 7 years. Now, depending upon where you have marked the 7 year cycles, above or below the line, on the opposite side mark the year of that age. e.g. If you were born in 1950 your first 7 year cycle would have 1957 either above or below the line.

Every seven years marks an important change in your personal development. See if you can line up the significant changes in your life with the dates on each 7 year cycle. For example: What year did you start school? Did you change schools at 7 years of age? When did you marry?

As you work on your time line you will find all kinds of things coming up from your memory bank, things you were not consciously aware of. Some of the things could be upsetting, but examine them carefully no matter how painful the process. You will discover quite a lot about why you do the seemingly irrational things you do now.

We all have pleasant memories and also unpleasant memories. We have to learn to face up to the unpleasant things without getting too emotionally involved in them.

SPRING CLEANING TIME. Once you start disturbing old memories it seems natural that you should feel guilty about things you did or did not do at the time. You cannot go back. You can only learn from the mistakes that you made; after all you did what you had to do at the time, you were not as developed as you are now. All you do is resolve never to make that mistake again.

This will be covered fully in a later lesson.

THINGS TO DO FOR THE WEEK.

1. I can do anything I think I can. Make a card— **I CAN IF I THINK I CAN.** Use this affirmation as often as you can during the day, particularly when you feel doubtful.

2. Look at your time line frequently and come to terms with your old memories. This is a MENTAL SPRING CLEANING.

Set aside one evening a week for revision of the previous lessons as well as the current one you are studying. You will be reinforcing all you are learning. THIS IS VERY IMPORTANT!

KEY 1. RECOGNITION.

SECTION 3. WHAT DO I BELIEVE?

The most important and essential thing that you need is a belief in yourself.

I BELIEVE IN MYSELF!

This is the theme of this section and it is one of the most important things you have to accept.

WHY SHOULD YOU BELIEVE IN YOURSELF?

It is very simple. If you do not believe in yourself no one else will.

It is essential to your happiness, success and fulfilment in life that you believe in YOU!

If you feel so depressed and discouraged about yourself remember this: there are others far worse off than you are, yet despite their setbacks and problems they believe in themselves and their goals.

All it takes is a little courage.

Say this simple statement: **I believe in myself.**

Say this at least twice a day, morning and evening particularly when you are about to go to sleep. Just drift off to sleep mentally saying these most important words. Say them gently without strain, rather like a lullaby. They will work wonders in your life.

Let's now talk about how you function as a human being. Very few people realise just how it is they function. They simply say, "I am alive aren't I?" and let it go at that.

There is so much more to it than that though, so let's have a stab at it. You are not just a body, you have a mind also and the most important part of you is your mind. Without your mind you would not be alive. You would simply be an inert lump of matter. Matter needs force and intelligence to animate it and these two aspects are from your mind.

This section will deal with how your mind works but of necessity it is only a simplified version. Your mind is a wonderful, complex mechanism that no human could possibly duplicate. The computer is the nearest thing man has made that is anything like it and that is only a pathetic copy.

Sufficient that you know you have a wonderful and extraordinary part of you that is so powerful you can change your whole life if you learn to use it properly.

YOUR MIND HAS THREE FUNCTIONS.

You only have one mind but it has three different aspects or functions. Psychologists have, for convenience, named these three functions the CONSCIOUS mind, the SUBCONSCIOUS mind and the SUPERCONSCIOUS mind.

THE CONSCIOUS MIND. This aspect of your mind is located in your head area. It is your intellect. Your five senses are here and these relay information about your surroundings to your brain. Once this information reaches the seat of consciousness in the centre of your brain you become aware of your surroundings. If you knock your shin against an obstacle the message is relayed along your nervous system to the brain which then relays it to the shin and you feel pain. You would not feel pain if the message did not reach the centre of consciousness. Anaesthetics and hypnosis submerge this centre.

You gather information about your environment through your five senses, sight, smell, sound, taste and touch. Your intellect works on all the data received. It analyses, reasons, draws on your memory bank for past information. All this is collated and then a decision is made. This decision is then passed on to your subconscious mind, the second phase of your mind. Your conscious mind is your reasoning mind, it chooses and makes decisions. Whatever you choose to do, for example, your work, your car, your home, whether to spend recklessly or save, these decisions are made by your conscious mind. It is the activity of this phase of the mind.

Your thinking is done with this phase of your mind and whatever you think automatically goes down into your subconscious mind. It is very important to remember the functions of each phase of your mind because there is a definite law at work here which determines what your life style will be. You are responsible for your own fortunes and your misfortunes and once you learn how your mind functions you can change your life.

The law of your mind is; "that according to whatever thoughts or ideas you hold in your conscious mind, these thoughts will bring a response or reaction from your subconscious mind." The thoughts and ideas conveyed to your subconscious mind become brain cell impressions and these are acted upon.

Your conscious mind is sometimes called your objective mind because it deals with outward objects. The objective mind recognises the objective world through your five senses. It is the director and your guide in your contact with your environment. You gain knowledge through your five senses and your objective or conscious mind learns through observing the environment, by your experiences in your environment, and by your education—not just academic but also your experiences of life. The greatest function of your objective mind or conscious mind is its reasoning capacity.

Your conscious mind is the 'guardian at the gate' and its special function is to protect your subconscious mind from false impressions.

Your thoughts are important as you will see, so make sure your thoughts are good, positive, constructive ones. You also have the power to choose what you think and what you believe about anything, choose wisely.

THE SUBCONSCIOUS MIND. The function of the subconscious mind is totally different from the function of the conscious mind.

The subconscious mind simply reacts to all the information sent by the conscious mind.

It is a receiver.

If you think with your conscious mind, "I'm a failure." your subconscious mind reacts to that statement and produces a failure feeling within you and you definitely feel a failure.

The subconscious mind (SCM for short), is situated from the heart to the navel. It is the seat of your emotions and your memory is stored there. This is the most important part of your mind. It controls all your involuntary bodily functions such as your heart beat, your breathing, your digestion and your glands etc.

You do not have to tell your heart to beat nor do anything about your breathing. Your wonderful SCM does all that for you. It never sleeps, it is on duty 24 hours a day, keeping you alive and functioning properly.

Whatever is put into it is acted upon. It cannot do anything else it can only react to what is put into it. It does not answer back and tell you if you make a wrong decision, it cannot.

Its only function is to obey orders.

The best analogy is to regard your CM (conscious mind) as the captain of the QE2. He is on the bridge and can see all the weather conditions and the state of the sea. His officers with him on the bridge use the various electronics and relay their findings to the captain who then makes a decision from all the data at his disposal. He then rings down his orders to the engine room. The engineers down below obey his orders implicitly. They do not answer back or feel the captain has made a mistake. They simply obey orders.

That is their function, to obey and carry out the captain's orders. They would put the lives of everyone on board at risk, including their own, if they did not obey.

The men in the engine room represent your subconscious mind. That is how you function.

Very simple isn't it?

Your CM gives the instructions and your SCM obeys them.

Your SCM reacts to the CM.

YOU ARE GIVING ORDERS TO YOUR SCM WHEN YOU DO THE EXERCISES.

All day long you are constantly giving orders to your SCM. Every thought you think eventually goes down there. So, what kind of thoughts are you harbouring about yourself right now? Do you say such things as, "I'm no good at that," or, "I'm not educated." and other similar things? Well, all that goes down and is firmly acted upon. A sobering thought, isn't it?

IT IS NOT YOUR FAULT.

From the day you were born you were subjected to all the beliefs and prejudices of everyone around you. You were programmed with all the limited beliefs of your ancestors. False beliefs and superstitions are handed down from generation to generation until someone makes a stand and decides not to be at the mercy of other peoples opinions and beliefs.

YOU HAVE FREEDOM OF CHOICE.

Now you are aware of how you function as a human being what are you going to choose? Are you going to choose to be happy, successful, prosperous, healthy and enthusiastic? Or, are you going to be at the mercy of all the negative thoughts and feelings that are already in your SCM? More about this next time.

THE SUPERCONSCIOUS MIND. The supconscious phase of mind (SPCM) is the source of inspiration in us. This activity functions from the crown of the head and it has direct access to the Universal life force which is everywhere present and is in everything including you and me! Sudden flashes of inspiration, a sudden perception, a hunch or intuitive leadings, telepathic and other extrasensory perceptions all function from this centre.

The superconscious activity of the mind can awaken and activate the most potent form of creative energy, the Universal life force, into the mind and body which can heal disease and produce conditions of success in every aspect of your life.

This power was used by the ancient Egyptians, the Babylonians and the Ancient Greeks with great mastery and was the secret of their successes.

Metaphysically it is known as the I Am, the Spirit of God

in us. People of the Old Testament affirmed Jehovah or I AM with great success and the people of the New Testament affirmed the name Jesus Christ or Christ Jesus with equal success.

It is the Divine in man, the Divine Intelligence or Infinite Intelligence.

Myrtle Fillmore, Co-Founder of the Unity Movement was given six months to live. She was dying of Consumption during the last century. She heard the words, "You are a child of God, you do not inherit sickness." From then on she began to call on Infinite Intelligence to guide her. These are her words:

"Life has to be guided by intelligence...Life is simply a form of energy and has to be guided and directed in man's body by his intelligence. How do we communicate with intelligence? By thinking and talking, of course."

She did just that. She talked to the living cells of her lungs. She apologised to her lungs for having called them weak and diseased. She thanked them for the work they were doing in keeping her alive. She praised them and called them good and she recognised the Infinite Intelligence within every cell of her body.

After working like this for a few weeks she began to feel better and from then on it was improvement all the way and two years later she was completely healed. This happened when she was in her forties and she lived a very active and fulfilling life for another forty years!

Most people have forgotten, or maybe they do not know, that we are three-fold in nature. We are body, mind and spirit. Our physical body is the outer expression, or manifestation, of our mind. We are mental and emotional beings and it is our thinking and feeling that dictates what we are in the outer manifestation.

You are a product of your intellect and your emotions. If you are aware of your spiritual identity and understand that spiritual does not mean religious, but is the most important part of your mind function, then you are on the way to a great new future.

This superconscious power can be released into your sub-conscious which is then relayed into your conscious mind by prayer, affirmations and meditation.

Try using the following affirmations:

"I am guided by Infinite Intelligence in every aspect of my life."

"Infinite Intelligence is in every atom and cell of my body and I am restored to wholeness."

"I am always successful in everything I do when Infinite Intelligence guides me."

The Ancients used the I AM with great success. The I AM produces a very powerful vibration of creative energy which brings about whatever you attach to this powerful statement. For example:

"I am sick." "I am very well."

Think about what you attach to this statement daily. Every cell in your body has a nucleus which is filled with living intelligence.

As you speak these words a vibration is set up which stimulates each body cell into either vibrant, constructive HEALTH OR, HARD DESTRUCTIVE CELLS WHICH CAUSE DISEASE.

PUT IT INTO PRACTICE.

1. Make a card with, I BELIEVE IN MYSELF. This must be used with the card you previously made for yourself, twice a day.

2. Get yourself a folder or a file and make notes that supplement these lessons.

3. Learn the three distinct aspects or functions of your mind.

This is very important. CM, SCM, and SPCM must be so familiar to you that you immediately respond when you see these initials or hear them spoken about.

LEARN THEM!

It is essential that you make a great effort at this stage, for unless you do this now you will not have a good grounding of the principles and your results will show this.

If you make 75% effort you will have 75% results. If you make 15% effort you get 15% results.

WHAT ABOUT 100%?

KEY 1. RECOGNITION.

SECTION 4. I AM TALENTED.

I am a wonderful, unique, creative being with talents and abilities I have yet to realise.

Deep within you are tremendous talents lying dormant, just waiting for you to discover them. They are locked in, unable to get out. They are waiting for you to release them.

If at any time you feel fed up, frustrated, don't know what to do with yourself, this section will give you the answers. BUT, you will have to work at it.

How do we know what our hidden talents are? The first thing we do is to take stock.

By now you should be aware that making your own notes as you go on through the course is a great help. It not only consolidates what you are learning but opens your mind to a new way of thinking about yourself.

What I am saying now is , that, you should come prepared with paper, pen, cards or anything else you think you may need. Of course it goes without saying that you should always have a mirror or a photograph at every study session. Also remember that I am personally involved with every student. As I type this I 'see' a great body of students around me, including YOU. I want you to know that I am speaking to you personally.

So now, let's start our stocktaking.

YOU NEED PEN, PAPER, MIRROR OR PHOTOGRAPH.

Study that face again. What are your thoughts now about yourself? Are you feeling a little better about yourself? There should be some small change in how you look at yourself. You should not be so easily put off by the reflection or the photograph. That is your first bit of success!

Now you are going to write down on your paper all the things you do well. In fact there should be two lists WORK type things and PLAY type things.

WORK TYPE THINGS. This list should incl
things, the skills that you use in your work, e.
electronics, machinery, tools, cooking utensils etc.

PLAY TYPE THINGS. These should include a
you do as a hobby, pastime, e.g. art, games, dancing, _l ∪ying
a musical instrument. etc.

Maybe you did something years ago that you no longer
do. That is a learned skill and if you enjoyed doing it, write
it down.

If you check your time line you will see things on it that
can refresh your memory.

These two lists should show you that you can do a lot of
things well.

THIS IS PART OF THE MIRROR
TECHNIQUE.

As you look in the mirror you will begin to say out loud all
the things you do well to the reflection or photograph. As
you do this a few times you will realise that there are a lot of
things you do well.

And, there are a lot more things that you can probably do
well. This exercise will help you to realise that the things
you do well far out weigh the things you cannot do, or think
you cannot do.

Take your time over this. The more you do it the stronger
you will feel.

DO NOT THINK ABOUT THE THINGS YOU
CANNOT DO. THERE ARE SO MANY MORE
THINGS THAT YOU CAN DO!

Whenever doubts occur keep telling yourself, "I can do......
and say the lists out loud. You know why you are doing this?

REINFORCEMENT. You are reinforcing all the things
you are thinking and saying about yourself and this will be
taken up by your subconscious mind (SCM) and worked on.

You are simply doing what was done to you in childhood

uy this time in reverse. You are saying good, positive things about yourself which is the truth about you.

You are recognising your own talents which have nothing to do with anyone else, they are uniquely yours.

By doing this regularly you will quickly begin to zoom in on the special talents and abilities that you possess.

YOU ARE SOMEONE SPECIAL! Because you are special you can make other people happy. Make a list of people to whom you are important.

Your family; workmates; neighbours; teachers; students; friends; shopkeepers; pets etc.

You are important to all these people because you can make them happy. Everyone on your list needs something from you. They need TLC.

Tender, loving care does not mean that you go overboard with false affection or sloppiness.

It simply means that you practice the GOLDEN RULE: Do to others what you would like others to do to you, but you do it first.

Smile at people; listen to what they say; speak pleasantly to them; show an interest in them. Do not wait for them to do it to you, you do it first!

You will make their day a lot brighter and you will feel a lot better and less sorry for yourself. You can never know the burdens other people are carrying which colour their attitudes toward everything and everyone they come in contact with.

ALL THOSE PEOPLE ON YOUR LIST ARE HAPPIER BECAUSE OF YOU!

If you want to be happy, make someone else happy!

REVISION.

1. Make a stocktaking list of all the things you do well.
2. Check your time line.
3. You are something special because you can make someone else happy.

4. Keep up the mirror technique and keep saying the affirmations.

ANSWER THE QUESTIONS AND PUT THEM IN YOUR FILE.

QUESTIONNAIRE.

1. What stops you from achieving your potential for greatness?
2. How do you limit the great power within you?
3. Why are you special?
4. Why is your list of NICE things about yourself important?
5. Why are your thoughts so important?
6. What does freedom of choice mean?
7. What does self development mean?
8. How has your time line helped you?
9. What is mental spring cleaning?
10. Why is it important to keep going back to the previous lessons?
11. Why should you believe in yourself?
12. Explain briefly what is meant by CM.
13. Explain briefly what is meant by SCM, and SPCM.
14. Why is it important to emphasise the things you do well?
15. Why is reinforcement so important?
16. What is TLC?
17. What is the GOLDEN RULE?
18. What should you do to be happy?
19. Is there any point that is unclear to you? If so, please go over the whole key again.

Please answer all questions. It is only by answering them can an assessment be made of your progress. There is to be no judgement made only an appraisal of your understanding. Remember, learning anything takes time and practice and patience (TPP).

YOU CAN DO IT!

SUNSPOTS

**IT IS NICE TO BE
IMPORTANT, BUT IT IS
IMPORTANT TO BE
NICE!**

Sunspots are little sayings or ideas which can be used as an affirmation at any time to reinforce other statements. You will be putting good things in your mind which will clean out the negative rubbish that is already in there.

KEY 2. WHAT DO I WANT?

SECTION 1. IS IT POSSIBLE?

Do you ever feel that you should have achieved a lot more than you have at this present moment Do you see other people who have apparently less talent, intelligence, skill and dedication passing you by? Have you ever felt that there must be something better for you than what you are now experiencing? What's wrong? Who is to blame for your low achievement at this point? Whose fault is it that you have not progressed as far or as fast as you felt you should?

Let's start by asking a question. "if other people in far worse circumstances than I am in right now can make it, then WHY CAN'T I?"

To answer this question you must first analyse the negative thought patterns and beliefs you have about yourself. These negative thoughts and feelings have been holding you back from realising your great potential. You must find the reasons for your inertia and put the blame where it belongs, before you can correct the situation.

First. Are you inclined to place the blame on a group or class of people who have a different creed or colour than you? If so, you are making a big mistake. There are too many other people in the same position who are succeeding despite prejudiced opposition.

Second. Do you blame the capitalistic society in which you live? Well consider this. The free enterprise system despite its faults, allows you the freedom to choose to try to become whatever it is you desire. It has faults, like any other system, but the alternatives are not as good.

Third. Do you blame your parents or the environment you were born into?

That is ridiculous. You have the same equipment as any other human being. Your mind is a fantastic, powerful, creative piece of equipment that no scientist can ever reproduce.

Fourth. It is the Establishment or the Government that

is to blame for lack of opportunity. Sorry! This is a negative generalisation which can never hold up. There are thousands and thousands of people today who are making great strides despite the Establishment or the Government, so that is an excuse.

YOU WILL NEVER SOLVE THE PROBLEM UNTIL YOU CORRECTLY PLACE THE BLAME.

Imprisoned in your mind are vast possibilities that have never had the chance to be realised. There is no power on earth greater than man's ability to dream, imagine and visualise. The greatest tragedy of all is to see human beings live, and eventually die, without ever having released the imprisoned power of a creative imagination.

From childhood we have put up barriers in our mind which act as a cage. We are imprisoned in this cage for the rest of our lives unless we do something about it. By working consistently with the exercises throughout this course of study you will break down the bars of the mental cage and feel what freedom truly means.

FEAR OF FAILURE. The biggest bar of all in your mental cage is fear of failure. Nothing blocks your dynamic creativity more than fear and human beings have many fears real or imagined.

The deepest need of all human beings is the need for self-esteem. A fear of failure is really a fear of being embarrassed. Instinctively we avoid exposing our self dignity to public ridicule. So, to avoid the possibility of disgracing ourselves we play safe by not even trying.

To loosen this negative bar from your cage remember that **IT IS NOT FAILURE THAT IS THE CRIME BUT YOUR LOW AIM!**

Real failure is not failing to reach your set goal, it is the failure to reach as high as you can. You can never really know if you have succeeded until you experience apparent failure. For example, a pole vaulter can never be certain if he has jumped as high as he possibly can until he knocks the bar down! So, keep raising your goals until you have a failure! Only then will you know that you have reached your peak. You have truly succeeded when you have seemingly failed.

SOLVE YOUR PROBLEMS OR YOUR PROBLEMS WILL DISSOLVE YOU Every problem is an opportunity to be creative. Let your problems be your motivation. The solution to every problem lies in the problem itself. Remember, if you are clever enough to imagine a problem then you are clever enough to discover a solution. You must use your creative imagination, release it from the cage of self-doubt and memories of old depressing failures. Today is the beginning of a new adventure. Imagine the exciting things that CAN HAPPEN TO YOU TODAY AND TOMORROW.

SELF CONFIDENCE Lack of self confidence is another bar of your mental cage. Lack of confidence will make you feel inferior. It will stop you trying something new. It will stop you thinking BIG. It will make you settle for second best.

YES, IT'S POSSIBLE!

Revive your dream. Maybe you once had a dream that someday you would achieve a certain thing. Then as time passed and other more pressing matters crowded in, the dream was shelved. Maybe you thought about it at odd times with regret and the thought, "It's not possible anyway."

IT IS POSSIBLE! Bring that dream out. Write it down. Look at it. Think about it. Keep going back to it and write down every idea that comes to you about it. Worry it. Keep at it.

THIS IS IMPORTANT! Let the ideas flow freely. Do not analyse or criticise anything at this stage. Everything is possible but you must give it a chance to develop. Criticism at this stage will stop the creative flow of your wonderful imagination. That will come later as you work out the form of your idea.

You know, many good ideas are dismissed as rubbish simply because the person who had the idea had such a low self-image he could not see the possibilities, the great potential.

Never underrate yourself. If everyone did that there would not have been the tremendous advances in medicine, science and technology during this century.

EVERYTHING IS POSSIBLE. NOTHING IS IMPOSSIBLE! Someone had a dream that man would walk on the moon. People said that it was impossible.

I was told that I would never be able to teach again after I injured my back. It took seven years to prove it was possible. It was not only possible, I also started my own business and worked twice as hard!

Begin to look at every idea as if it were possible. Make a game of t. Keep it light-hearted. This will avoid anxiety and strain and more and more ideas will begin to flow freely.

Call it THE IDEA GAME. Play it every day. Let it be a form of doodling at first. Wonderful things will begin to happen.

TRUST YOUR IDEA. You have the same creative imagination as all the great thinkers have and look what they come up with!

The more you say, IT IS POSSIBLE, the stronger this will become in your SCM and once this has taken root in the fertile SCM area it will be acted upon and good things will begin to happen outwardly.

Good positive, powerful suggestions to your SCM, that everything is possible, will give you the impetus you require.

This is self-motivation. For years other people have motivated you with negative words, failure words which you accepted unknowingly. You are now changing all that.

QUESTIONS TO ASK YOURSELF ABOUT YOUR IDEAS.

1. Is it a practical idea?
2. Has it been done before?
3. Is it better than similar ideas?
4. Is it honest?
5. Will it help others?

Remember: I BELIEVE IN MYSELF!

KEY 2. WHAT DO I WANT?

SECTION 2. IS IT PROSPERITY?

Let's begin by defining prosperity.

The word prosperity comes from the Latin root which translates—according to hope, or, to go forward hopefully. So it is not so much a condition in life but rather an attitude toward life.

Prosperity is an attitude of mind, it is a way of living and thinking and it is not just money or things.

By contrast, poverty is an attitude of mind, it is a way of thinking and living and it is not just a lack of money or things.

Prosperity means total well-being. It covers health, love, peace, harmony, good relationships, as well as abundance of material things. It means every good thing that you can experience in your life. However, good starts with your own thinking. If you have good thoughts about yourself and others, then you reap the benefits in your own life.

From childhood you have been conditioned to believe that your life is shaped by what happens around you and to you.

Your life is not lived by what happens 'out there'. It is lived from inside yourself, inside your own mind. It is what you think, what you say and what you do about what happens 'out there' that matters.

Before you can have prosperity in your own life you must accept complete responsibility for your own thoughts and feelings, your own words and deeds.

This is the starting point for taking control of your own life.

You are not responsible for the forecasts and predictions of others no matter how professionally qualified they are. In the current economic situation where the valve of money is constantly fluctuating the doom and gloom prophets abound. These so-called experts cannot decide how you feel about the financial state of the country and certainly not about your own personal finances.

You are responsible for your own thinking and your own feelings and this responsibility must be taken seriously.

If you want to change your life and particularly your prosperity then your attitude towards yourself and other people has to change.

Make a start by refusing to see yourself as poor, unemployed, failing at work or business. You are none of these things, they have no place in your life from this point on.

To prosper means that you begin to advance in all aspects of your life. You grow and unfold spiritually, intellectually, emotionally, socially and financially.

It is normal and natural for you to have the desire to improve yourself and your circumstances; for you to desire prosperity, success, achievement and recognition in your life.

You should have all the money you need to do all the things you want to do, when you want to do them.

You were born with all the equipment necessary to lead a full, happy and successful life.

You were born to win; to rise above all obstacles; to express all the wonderful talents, beauty and abilities within you.

You are not here to earn a meagre living. You are not here to live in poverty.

Emerson says, 'you are born to be rich or inevitably to grow rich by the use of your faculties.' In other words, you must use what you have, the talents that you possess. If you don't use then you lose them!

By your wrong thinking you frustrate the talents and abilities you have. The great potential within you atrophies and dies and so do you.

Most physical illness is psychosomatic, the outer manifestation of an inner disordered state of mind. We must also recognise that any financial lack or limitation is also the outer manifestation of an inner distorted state of mind.

Start right now to eliminate such thoughts as, 'I can't,' 'I'm afraid,' 'there is not enough to go round,' 'the rich have it all,' etc. Start to think about abundance and sufficiency for everyone. Keep yourself centred in the creative power within you keeping your thoughts positive and creative. KEEP MOVING IN THE DIRECTION OF YOUR DREAM!

Poverty is a disease, it is a disease of the mind. It is the cancer of society. If people only realised that poverty is a state of mind they could quickly do something to change their lot. Poverty destroys humanity. It fills prisons and it is a dirty, degrading, disgusting experience. The anxiety, worry, strain and tension caused by poverty is responsible for 90% of the illness of humans.

Throughout the ages the poor were told by religious leaders that it was virtuous to be poor, they would get their reward in the afterlife. The hungry, starving masses of people were kept in order this way. As the church preached this doctrine the rich got richer and the poor got poorer. WE ALL CARRY IN OUR SCM THE OLD RACE BELIEFS OF LONG AGO!

It is normal and natural to desire to be rich! Unless you are rich, (and that means rich ideas that you will carry out with joy and enthusiasm) you will not be very much good to yourself or to others.

It is abnormal not to desire riches and prosperity in your life.

Many people feel that prosperity is divinely damned and that poverty is spiritually approved. They quote Jesus as saying, 'You cannot serve God and mammon'.

They should stop using God as an excuse for their own failures! Mammon—riches regarded as an object of worship or false god.

Money is not the root of all evil, it is the LOVE OF MONEY which is the root of all evil.

Money is a symbol, a means of exchange. If you worship money to the detriment of everything else you will suffer and lose the money you have. Money has to circulate it should not be hoarded for a rainy day—your rainy day will surely come if you do! Money should be used for good purposes, to get the good things of life you need for comfort. It should not be wasted or squandered.

We live in a rich universe, an opulent universe, there is no shortage. It is our own belief in shortage which causes envy, jealousy and a coveting of someone else's prosperity.

There is more than enough to go round. There is no need to envy or steal from others.

We live in a universe of law and order. There are principles or laws by which all our experiences, conditions and events take place. There is a definite law of cause and effect in everything.

The law of life is the law of belief. The science of getting rich is based on the law of belief. It is your belief which makes the difference between wealth and poverty; between success and failure; between health and sickness.

IT IS A COSMIC LAW:

Like thoughts produce like effects.

You are not here by chance, you are here to find your true place in life; to give of your talents to the world; to expand, unfold and grow in a wonderful way according to your great inner potential.

You are not here just to earn a living. You are here to express life and to give your hidden talents and abilities to the world through your mind, body and soul. Your desire for happiness, health, peace of mind, prosperity and true place in life is really the urging, prompting and the inclination of the living intelligence within you seeking expression through you. Your desire right now should be to make the most of yourself.

You are living in a wonderful age, an age of opportunity. You must determine to go with the current of life and not swim against the tide if you want to make the most of the opportunities which are everywhere.

3 STEPS TO RICHES.

1. Never make a negative statement about your finances. For example,

"I can't get a job."

"Business is bad."

Instead, make a positive statement to weaken and dissolve the negative, for example,

"Work is everywhere if I want it."

"I am now guided to the right work for me at this moment."

"Business is booming."

2. Repeat as often as possible the two words, **wealth, success.**

You will be filling your mind with good, positive statements which will slowly dilute the old negative thought, patterns which keep you down and stop you rising to your higher level of understanding.

Here is an affirmation to repeat as often as you can:

"MY DEEPER SELF, HIDDEN IN MY SCM PRESENTS ME WITH NEW, CREATIVE IDEAS OF PROSPERITY NOW!"

3. Lull yourself to sleep giving thanks for the new, rich ideas that are constantly coming to you. Feel a sense of gratitude to your SCM as you drift off to sleep. That works wonders! You do already have a lot to be thankful for.

Whatever you have in your mind when you are in a drowsy state will go straight down into your SCM and it will be acted upon.

If you desire more money then you must have a money consciousness.

Your consciousness is your awareness at this time. It is not static, It is constantly growing as you go from one experience to another.

If you were brought up to be thrifty with money that will be your present consciousness. If you saw people around you wasting money you will automatically waste money without even thinking about it.

I have a very rich friend who was taught as a child to only buy what she needed. She saw her parents giving to charity on a regular basis and she was encouraged to do this also. Her father's business flourished and so did her chosen career. She was taught to be honest, caring about others and to give thanks for what she had. This policy is the business ethic she also teaches her staff.

Where is your money consciousness at this moment?

Just how rich can you envision yourself as being?

"I am money conscious." Say this constantly particularly just before you go to sleep.

To be rich you must have a rich consciousness.

Think rich. Make good prosperous mental pictures of what you want in your life. See yourself as living in a rich way and all that this means to you.

Give a money command to your SCM.

"Make a million." "Make a thousand." "Make a hundred." or, whatever amount you are comfortable with.

Use money to attract money.

Have a money bookmark. Use a five pound note as a bookmark and each time you handle it as you find your place, examine it lovingly and imagine your wallet or purse is full to over f lowing with these notes.

Make out a cheque to yourself for a large sum of money, the sum you can accept in your consciousness. Sign it, The Universal Banker. Use this as a bookmark or put it with your accounts etc.

By working with these exercises you are making money conscious brain cell impressions. Like attracts like and your money thoughts will attract money to you.

Keep quiet about all this. You will weaken your resolve if you talk about it at this stage. Other people will not understand, but they will soon see the difference for themselves.

Never be tempted to abuse this inner power that you have, it will only work against you if you do!

Coin exercise.

Take 3 silver coins, all the same denomination, 3x50, 3x20, 3x10, 3x5. Hold them in one hand.

Put one of the coins into the empty hand and as you do so

say in a commanding voice, MAKE A MILLION, MAKE A THOUSAND, or whatever sum you feel happy with. Say this 3 times. Do the same with each coin until they are all in the other hand.

Now repeat this, transferring them back again. Remember, say forcefully the affirmation 3 times with each coin transfer.

AND NOW DO IT ONCE MORE. You will have transferred the coins three times and you will have said the affirmation 3 times with each coin.

Do this for at least 28 days.

You will become more money conscious, you will think rich, and that is how you attract money. You are impressing your SCM. Your thoughts will become your future.

THINK RICH, YOU WILL ATTRACT RICHES.

Affirm: My prosperity is unlimited, my success is unlimited now! I am rich, well and happy and every aspect of my life is in order.

Once your money consciousness expands and you begin to see an improvement in your finances you should also be aware that you have a responsibility to share what you have. It is a natural law to give and receive. But you must do the giving first.

Giving and Receiving.

Our very existence depends upon this law. As a baby you had to give something of yourself to get what you wanted. You yelled, the only thing you could do at that stage of development, for food and comfort.

Throughout your life you are constantly giving before you receive. You must ask for whatever it is you want at any given time, you must put forth your views before you can be acknowledged, you must give kindness if you would receive kindness, give love before you can receive it.

You must give before you can get.

How does this apply to prosperity?

As with everything else you give before you receive and

the usual way of giving is through tithing. Tithing is an ancient custom which most wealthy people practise today. One tenth of their income is given to charity or the Church or to educate others less fortunate. It is a matter of personal choice as to where the tithe goes, but giving to the person or organisation who inspired you and helped you is what most people do as they know the money will be used to expand the lives of others.

Remember that to give is the first step to receiving, it is a natural law which has been proved since man began to realise that more good comes through giving that anything else.

A practical way to look at it is like this: If your income is £150 a week then before you do anything else you give one tenth, £15 to the person or organisation who inspired you and you know will use the money for the betterment of others.

Giving in this way must be done in a thankful spirit. You are grateful for all that you have and all that you hope to have in the future. You are giving back something of what you have received.

And the more you give the more you receive.

When I first discovered that giving was a prosperity law I felt I did not have enough to give even though I recognised that the principle was a sound one.

My teacher at that time was a very wise person and when I said that all my money was needed and I couldn't spare anything yet, I couldn't afford to tithe, she smiled and said, "You can't afford not to tithe."

She asked me if I had a savings account. At that time I had an arrangement with my bank that £5.00 would go into a savings account at the end of each month and that if I ever overdrew my account this could be used to cover the resulting debt.

She asked me if I missed that money. Well I had to say I didn't, as it had become part of my regular outgoings. I never thought of it as savings.

I was then told to tithe in the same way. Do it automatically each month as though it was a regular outgoing. To give with thanksgiving and without any doubts at all that this tithe would multiply a thousandfold.

I couldn't believe it but I did it. At first I began to resent the tenth of my income going out, and it took a few months for me to realise that I had to reorganise my spending to include this.

I slowly began to realise that I had wasted a lot of money by impulse buying and not keeping an account of my spending. That was the turning point for me. I became organised in my spending and that alone gave me something to spare each month. It also meant that not only was I never in debt but that my savings grew. My money awareness grew from then on. I carefully planned my finances and the first year I had enough to pay for a holiday for the family. My haphazard money management had deprived us of holidays for a few years!

Since then I have gone from strength to strength for I not only tithe one tenth of my income but everything else I receive. I support an education programme for children and I give to the religious organisation from which I receive inspiration and various charities.

A large majority of the people today do not realise the importance of tithing. The general attitude is 'what's in it 'for me?' It is not confined just to undividuals but also to communities and nations.

Everything starts with the individual and we must start with ourselves. The law is:

YOU CANNOT GET SOMETHING FOR NOTHING.

We must give before we get.

When I first started tithing I did not believe my teacher wholeheartedly. I just could not see that my tithe would return a 'thousandfold' After five years of regular tithing I found that this was indeed true, for everything I had tithed was returned a thousandfold and my bank statements proved this.

An important point to remember is that you cannot give grudgingly. What you give must be given with a generous spirit and with faith and thankfulness for what you already have. And know, without a shadow of a doubt, that your giving has created a vacuum which will be filled to overflowing.

Work on that for a few weeks and see what happens. If nothing much seems to be happening at first do not despair. Just realise that things are happening but any doubts will block the flow.

To prove this law you must give it time. Your SCM needs time to work on these principles and also time to clear out the negative thoughts and feelings you may still have stored away from childhood.

If there is any difficulty with this portion of the lesson, leave it until you have worked through the rest of the book, then come back to it with a greater depth of understanding.

It all takes time and you will prove this and all the other things as I have, if you persevere.

YOU CAN DO IT IF YOU TRY!

KEY 2. WHAT DO I WANT?

SECTION 3. IS IT HEALTH?

The natural, normal state of every human being is perfect health. Unfortunately, the vast majority of humans are decidedly unhealthy. Why? It is because they do not understand how human beings function. Man is not a body containing a mind, he is a mind operating through a body.

The body of itself is the result of the activity of Mind; it is molded by Mind and it is changed by Mind.

This is the fundamental truth or reality of human existence.

IF YOU CHANGE YOU MENTAL STATE YOU CHANGE YOUR PHYSICAL STATE.

A sudden sense of fear causes the face to turn grey. Also, a sudden sense of shame causes the face to turn red or flush. The scientific explanation for this is that the contraction and dilation of blood vessels are under the control of the vasomotor nerves and these nerves are influenced by emotions.

So, the more angrily or fearfully we react to people or situations the more we weaken our physical bodies.

It has been proved that mental states can cause muscle tension which contributes to Rheumatoid Arthritis, because of the increased pressure on joints; or to low blood sugar because of the increased use of sugar in muscular contraction; or to hyperventilation; or to chronic low back pain; or to severe neck pain.

Dr. Sellers from UCLA after many experiments and tests says that anger and anxiety and other emotional stresses may make it possible for virus infection, including polio, to enter the brain more easily. Such emotions release two body chemicals, adrenalin and serotonin, which help break down the body's strong, natural defences.

HOW CAN MIND HAVE SO MUCH POWER?

Man does not think only with his brain, he thinks with his whole body. Each separate, tiny cell is a spark of Mind. There is not a single point in the entire universe that is not indwelt by Mind. And there is not a single atom in the body that is at any moment separated from mental action.

We are so used to thinking of two worlds, the physical world and the mental world that it is hard to conceive of them both being one.

That which the mind thinks the body thinks; that which the body thinks, it becomes. Every mental condition records itself in the body and as the mind changes there is a corresponding change in the body, an exact reflection of the changed thought.

ILLNESS IS DISTORTED THOUGHT.

Illness is some distorted idea that has become dominant.

It is not true to say that illness is "caused by the mind."

The distorted physical form that we call 'illness' is the distorted thought-form in a visible state.

The problem is one of *thought.* The solution is the same. Change the thought and you change the condition.

Many people cling to their illness. It is a way of getting sympathy, of getting attention. They have the freedom of choice in this—they choose to hang on to the illness, they are willing martyrs.

The control of sickness is mental because sickness itself is mental.

Sickness is—as Freud said—simply a shadow of the mind. The body itself has no power to generate sickness.

A healthy mind will shadow forth a healthy body.

An unhealthy mind will shadow forth an unhealthy body.

Every new cell created in the body is either a positive or a negative thought in form. The cell is the thought itself.

IMPORTANT?

Healthy thoughts mean healthy cells. Sick thoughts mean sick cells.

We can better understand this when we realise that cells are created as quick as lightning. The red blood corpuscles are built at the rate of 1,000,000 a second, and they normally pass on at the same rate.

If you multiply this with the other parts of the body you can see this 'body' is really a whirling dynamo of thought energy, mind ceaselessly falling into form.

Every atom of your being is a miniature universe. It is a light surrounded by lesser lights in perpetual motion.

Sickness is the outer evidence of an inner disturbance.

Health on the other hand is the outward sign of an integrated mind.

If we think good, constructive thoughts then our body responds likewise.

If we envy, criticize, condemn, hate or resent other people then this will show in *our* body and affairs. It will not hurt them! Watch what you say about yourself. If you feel a bit off colour do you say such things as :

"I have flu."

"I caught a cold."

"I feel sick."

"I have a headache."

Oh! no you don't!

You have a distorted thought-form manifesting as a cold, flu, a headache etc.

Start to correct yourself whenever you say things like this. Start thinking and saying the opposite. Think about and say the solution to the problem instead of repeating the problem over and over. By constant repetition you programme your SCM so by constantly thinking and saying the solution you programme your mind with the truth.

Constantly thinking and speaking about something, whether good or bad, gives the thing power. It then becomes so magnified in your mind it will manifest as a serious illness.

Start thinking and saying the opposite to the above:

"I am well."

"I feel good."

"I never catch cold."

"I never get headaches."

You are speaking the truth when you say these things. Your natural state is perfect health. **IT IS NOT NATURAL TO BE SICK OR ILL.**

You are focusing on the solution instead of dwelling on the negative thought-form.

Solutions to any discomforts etc.

Repeat these as often as you can whenever you feel discomfort. Many students repeat them over and over until they feel better. Some repeat them as many as 50 or 60 times without stopping! It's all up to you as an individual. You have freedom of choice. Remember, the more effort you put into this the greater the results.

I feel healthy

I feel happy

I feel terrific!

I am strong, fit and healthy, my body knows it and my body shows it!

If you work on these solutions each time you feel uncomfortable you will find that you need never take aspirins, pills, cigarettes or alcohol.

* If you are a smoker you should drink plenty of water each day; take three deep breaths at a time out of doors; and take vitamin B complex capsules—one a day.

Also say things like, "Smoking makes me feel sick. Smoking ruins my appearance. Smoking is simply burning money. I do not need to smoke because I feel good."

Epidemics are caused by people believing in them. What you believe becomes a reality in your life. First there is an announcement on the radio or TV about a flu epidemic. Immediately people start worrying about it and hoping they will not fall victim. They notice people at work feeling unwell and the word spreads that Flu has arrived. They sniff a bit and say they have Flu. Of course there are some people who never get Flu, I am one of them. I do not believe in epidemics. I know I am healthy and fit and I say so.

I do not accept the opinions of other people. I draw my own conclusions from the evidence before me and I know the power of suggestion, so I make sure I counteract any negative statements with positive ones.

My students say I always look fantastically healthy and they wish they could look that way. They can!

Remember, the choice is yours. If you want to be healthy then think and express health constantly.

Students frequently tell me, with great pride, that nearly all the members of their office or work place have become sick with flu, but they did not get it. They were doing something right! They refused to give in to the beliefs of other people. They did not want flu and they worked at that with perfect results.

Suggestions from other people are insidious, we unknowingly accept them and they go straight into our SCM. As a result, they come up into our conscious mind, we realise them, and accept them because our peer group feels strongly about them. This happens because we are 'off guard' so to speak. We must be very vigilant and should analyse all we see and hear carefully to see if it is positive or negative, then we can take the proper precautions. Learn to be 'on guard' whenever you are listening or seeing anything. Do not judge by appearances, for things are never what they seem.

RECAP!

Positive thoughts and positive words become healthy cells in your body. So keep cheerful and smile when things seem to go wrong.

Do not be tempted to give in to depressing, negative thoughts, as this will produce unhealthy and distorted cells in your own body.

Learn not to react immediately to a negative situation,

pause a little before replying. This will give you a chance to think in the right way.

If you want to be healthy, think healthy thoughts!

Affirm:

'I am young, fit and healthy, my body knows it and my body shows it.'

'I always keep my thoughts positive for I know I am a product of what I think."

'Infinite Intelligence guides me in everything I do and I am always successful.'

I have a healthy mind and body.'

KEY 2. WHAT DO I WANT?

SECTION 4. IS IT PEOPLE?

People are a power in your life. They ether build you up or they put you down.

People are important to you. There is no way you can do without them. You need them.

You can never get away from people. It is the interaction with family, friends, neighbours, workmates, casual acquaintances, in fact everyone you meet on a daily basis, which gives you the impetus, and the challenge for growth.

We learn a great deal from people. They are a mirror image which reflects what we really are. If we see faults in the people we come into contact with, we should stop right there and say, "This fault is in me."

You are subconsciously recognising a particular thing; in yourself that needs working on. This takes courage to recognise your own faults. Don't ignore this bit because it makes you feel a trifle uncomfortable. Work at it. It will give you such a great insight into yourself and you will be amazed how you will begin to understand other people.

We can only be aware of our own faults when we see them reflected in other people or if other people tell us. We don't like that either!

Also remember that what we admire in other people is in us!

People reflect to us the things we need to come to terms with.

We can never get away from people so we must learn to get along with them.

If we start with ourselves then we are better able to understand what makes other people tick.

All people—and that includes YOU.—have basic needs, which if not fulfilled will cause a great deal of trouble.

We need love, acceptance, praise and encouragement, comfort and caring, and a goal to strive for.

These needs will be dealt with fully as we work through

the course. At this time we will deal with how to develop skill with people.

When you have a proper understanding of human nature and people you can become a very skillful manager of people. I said manager of people, not manipulator of people.

Understanding people and human nature simply involves recognising people for what they are—not what you think they are or what you want them to be!

THE PRIMARY INTEREST OF ALL PEOPLE IS THEMSELVES!

This goes for you as well. You are more interested in yourself than in any other person in the world.

Man's nature is self interest, You should not become embarrassed by this, it is the way we are, the way we have always been and the way we will always be. **It is not selfish** to think of yourself in this way. It is a fact of nature.

Remember, man's actions are governed by self thought, self-interest. This is so strong in man that the dominant thought in giving to charity is the satisfaction or pleasure that the giver gets from giving, not the good the gift will do, that comes second!

Four words will turn people away from you when talking together.

I, ME, MY, MINE. When you talk to people about yourself you are rubbing them up the wrong way and you are working against human nature.

On the other hand:

YOU, YOUR. Is talking to them about themselves, is rubbing them up the right way and working with human nature.

When you talk to people about themselves they are deeply interested and absolutely fascinated. They will think very highly of you for doing this. You are talking about their favourite subject.

I have proved this so many times, and you will get a deeper understanding of human beings and I can assure you it is not boring, it is fascinating.

If you can give up the satisfaction YOU get from talking about YOURSELF then your efficiency, your personality, your influence and power will be greatly increased.

When you talk to others talk about them and get them talking about themselves. This makes you an interesting conversationalist!

As we mentioned previously man needs to feel important and to be recognised.

So, the more important you make people feel the more they will respond to you. Everybody wants to be treated as a somebody. No one wants to be treated as a nobody. When they are ignored or talked down to then they are being treated as a nobody, a person of no importance.

The other person is just as important to himself as you are to yourself. An important way to make people feel important is to LISTEN to them. The more you listen, the more knowledgeable you will become, the better you will be liked, and the better conversationalist you will be. People love a good listener. Why? Because a good listener always allows people to hear their favourite speaker, THEMSELVES

RULES FOR BEING A GOOD LISTENER.

1. Look at the person who is speaking. Anyone worth listening to is worth looking at.

2. Ask questions. This shows that you are really listening.

3. Lean towards the speaker and listen intently to what is being said. It will appear as though you don't want to miss a single word.

4. Stick to the speaker's subject when asking questions. (asking questions is a high form of flattery) and don't interrupt the speaker, wait for a pause.

5. Use the speakers words—YOU and YOUR. If you use I, Me, or MINE, you are switching the focus from the speaker to yourself. That is talking, not listening.

A HAPPINESS FORMULA.

Every day say one kind thing to at least three people. Then see how you feel for having done that!

Smile at everyone with whom you come into contact during the day, whether you know them or not. A smile can lighten a heavy load and you can never know the burdens other people carry around in their minds.

ALWAYS SAY THANK YOU. It makes people feel appreciated.

BE GENEROUS WITH SINCERE PRAISE.

Look for somebody and something to praise, then do it!

Praise the act, not the person. This will avoid embarrassment and confusion and it creates an incentive for more of the same act.

Do not criticise unless you have to. Make the criticism impersonal, criticise the act not the person.

There is more joy in giving than in receiving. When you see the happiness and gratitude and pleasure you bring to others by showing in a small way that you care about them, YOU will feel good.

QUESTIONS.

1. Where in the four sections can you place the blame for your seeming lack of achievement?
2. What is the deepest need of all human beings?
3. What is real failure?
4. Why do we say that every problem is an opportunity?
5. Why are many good ideas dismissed as rubbish?
6. What is true prosperity?
7. Why is poverty a sin?
8. What makes the difference between wealth and poverty?
9. Do you have a rich money consciousness?
10. What is the natural, normal state of each human being?
11. How can mind have so much power regarding your health?
12. How can you programme your SCM for good health?
13. Why are people a power in your life?
14. What are the basic needs of all human beings
15. What are man's actions governed by?
16. Why should you talk to people about themselves?
17. What is a good way to make people feel important?

SUNSPOTS

**MY PROBLEMS ARE
ONLY MOLEHILLS THAT
I CAN STEP OVER
EASILY—THEY ARE NOT
MOUNTAINS THAT I
HAVE TO CLIMB!**

KEY 3. WHO IS DRIVING?

SECTION 1. CIRCUMSTANCES?

Do you feel that circumstances are beyond your control? That situations are forced upon you?

Do you say such things as :

"It's alright for them."

"I never had the chance."

"I never had the opportunity."

...and there are lots more like these.

All these sayings are excuses, or alibies. These are the things we say when faced with an opportunity to try something new or when we see other people pass us by up the stairway of success.

Let us look a little closer at some of these things and maybe you will be able to relate to something in them which can give you the motivation to really start changing your life.

Living in the past. If we constantly look back to past events whether they were successes or failures we are allowing ourselves to stagnate.

A stagnant pool is choked with weeds and stinks; so your mind is choked with garbage and it also stinks!

The pool needs clear, running water to give it new life and health so that it can flourish. Your mind needs clear, constructive thoughts to wash out the garbage so that new ideas can come in.

Whatever your circumstances were when you were younger than you are now, no matter what opposition you faced, it no longer matters.

Why do we alibi?

We come back to the fear of failure, remember?

"You can't do that."

Blaming circumstances or other people only weakens our resolve to have a try.

I'm too old now. Rubbish! What has a number got to do with it? Throughout the country there are 70 and 80 year old people of both sexes who are studying for and getting degrees in a wide range of subjects. They missed out when they were younger, but the determination to go for their secret dream spurred them on to victory. A woman in her 70s still races her power boat at high speeds and wins!

Older people from all walks of life are getting on with the art of living.

A man of 70 is still working full time at a very demanding job and he still makes time to drive up and down the country at weekends, and is learning to play the guitar!

A 96 year old lady was doing her own housework and helping other people until she was taken seriously ill at 93. Doctors said she would not recover and her relatives prepared for the worst. She showed 'em! She not only fully recovered but she writes, embroiders beautiful pictures and knits beautiful things for anyone without payment. She loves to help in anyway she can. Her attitude is fantastic. She loves looking after the old ladies (they are 60 and 70 year olds who look and act older than she is). She loves life and life repays her abundantly.

All these people have one thing in common. A determination to live life to the full. They are happy, healthy, prosperous, fulfilled people who love life and living. They all see life as a wonderful opportunity for growth.

Only one of the above mentioned people was born into a family that had wealth. All the others came from ordinary backgrounds with little formal education, but the challenges they met were all taken in their stride as something they had to get on with. They did not complain, they just got on with what they had to do and did it cheerfully.

A past student was unemployed when he came to our classes some years ago. He had no education having truanted a lot. We got down to setting a goal. He announced that his goal was to be a millionaire in five years.

The class hooted with laughter, they thought he was joking, especially the young executives who were also attending at the time. He was serious. We discussed ways in which he could achieve that ambition.

First he had to decide exactly what he was most interested in. Then, he needed some education. So he enrolled at night school for a course in English and Maths.

His next step was to find a job to get himself into the work habit. He found employment: sweeping a factory floor. He gave of his best to this job. He wasn't concerned about his low pay or status, he became interested in keeping that factory floor spotless and doing extra little jobs as he saw them. The boss was very impressed with his attitude and began to give him small responsibilities.

He studied a particular aspect of the work and asked many questions about it. He was then asked if he would like to try his hand in this department. Again he showed the same enthusiasm for learning all he could about the job, He finished the course with us and months went by. He telephoned to say he had an opportunity to take a market stall at weekends selling books and bric-a-brac. Nothing more was heard of him until two years ago. Quite out of the blue he rang to say he was going abroad to live and he asked if he could come and see me. I did not recognise the tall, handsome, well-dressed man who greeted me warmly.

"Well," he said smiling at me, "I made it, I am a millionaire."

He pulled from his breast pocket a rather grubby, folded piece of paper. Carefully he opened it out and showed it to me, It was his goal chart which I had given to him over five years ago. The entry in the long term section was: "I am a millionaire now in my realisation. In 5 years' time my stepping stones will have created it. Thank you."

He gently folded the paper back into its original folds and put it back into his pocket.

"That's my mascot. It will always remind me to go inside myself first to get the ideas and then follow them up. I will be teaching my children to do the same."

Off he went, a changed man. He had struggled very hard over the years, but the thing that kept him going was the knowledge that he had the power within himself to either make or break his own life—it was his responsibility to get on doing the things he knew he must do, (his stepping stones), to get what he wanted. He knew no one else could ever do it for him, he could either stay as he was or work at getting what he wanted.

We also have the power within us to change our lives but we must stick at it. Perseverance is the name of the game.

YOU CAN DO IT!

THINGS TO DO!

Take time to assess the information given and see which of it relates to your own particular circumstances. Do not dismiss this by thinking it does not apply to you if you are very young.

It applies to everyone, young and so called old!

The younger you are when you start working to enhance your life the better you will be because you have many more years to carry on working for all that you desire in your life.

The number is not important. What you believe is very important for that is the thread on which your life hangs.

Think carefully about what motivates the people mentioned. Remember, if you have a desire to change something in your life then that is all you need as motivation.

The next section will deal with setting goals. So what you do now is preparation for your own goal-setting.

Your consciousness at this moment in time will decide what your main goal in life will be. That is all you have to work with at this point. You must feel happy with the goals you set otherwise you will never attain them.

Careful thought now will save you a lot of time later on!

KEY 3. WHO IS DRIVING?

SECTION 2. START THE DAY RIGHT.

Today is where it all is at. Not yesterday or tomorrow, but today, right here and now. There is only NOW. We are forever functioning in the NOW. Yesterday has gone, never to return; tomorrow has yet to come and it will always be coming. You live in the NOW and you will always live in the NOW.

All that being so, then we have to make the best of the NOW. It is our only opportunity to do whatever we want to do.

Procrastination. This is the thief of time. When you 'put off' until tomorrow what you should be doing today time has gone never to return. That means an opportunity is lost. You will never feel the same as you do at this moment, so if there is something you need to do then do it when you think of it, because you can never retrace your steps.

There is only NOW! What you do now is very important. What you think now is very important. Your thoughts and actions today become the happenings of tomorrow.

You decide your own day. If you choose to think positive, constructive thoughts your actions will be the same. If you choose to harbour negative, destructive thoughts then your actions will correspond. Whatever you choose today manifests tomorrow. That, my friend, is a very sobering thought is it not?

Lets's imagine! You are just waking up in bed after a good night's sleep. As you gradually become aware of your surroundings you realise it is Monday morning and you have to get up for work. Immediately, you feel quite depressed. In your mind you go through the problems that you know await at work. There's the boss; the irritations you get from your workmates ; the things you have to catch up on, etc, etc. You slowly drag yourself out of bed and open the curtains.

It's raining.

Bleakly you look out at the grey sky and your heart sinks into your feet. You know, without a shadow of a doubt, that today is going to be one hell of a day.

"I hate Mondays," you mutter to yourself as you rush around getting dressed.

You can't find a clean pair of socks, or tights. You rush downstairs fill the kettle, put the bread in the toaster as you finish dressing. You realise you have to get the things you need to take with you, so you collect your stuff and rush to make coffee. The smoke arising from the toaster and the smell tells you that the toast is burned. You rescue it but who wants black toast?

Your watch tells you that you are late. Out of the house you dash. The car wont start. A good curse doesn't help. You finally leave and join the endless queue of rush hour traffic. Fuming in your car you wait. Eventually you arrive at work. Late.

The sarcasm of the boss does not help. Neither does the snide remark from the 'know-it-all'. Your day continues like this. You breathe a sigh of relief at the end of the day and you certainly do not look forward to the homeward journey.

"I knew it was going to be a bad day," you mutter to yourself or anyone else who is passing.

That is one heck of a way to start any day, is it not?

The biggest majority of people do start their day in a similar way.

Let's start again.

It is Monday morning and you have just awakened. You take time to stretch your arms above your head, rather like a cat stretches itself after sleep. You recall that it is Monday morning and you have a feeling of anticipation about what today will bring.

You slowly get out of bed and draw back the curtains to reveal a rainy day. For a few moments you watch the rain splash against the window and hear the patter of the raindrops. The sky is grey but as you look up at it you know, without a shadow of a doubt, that above the grey cloud layer there is a bright blue sky and a shining sun. You know this because you have seen it when you flew high above the clouds in a plane.

"Well, this rain will soon pass and the sun will shine," you say to yourself as you wash, dress and make the breakfast.

You enjoy your food and you clear away the dishes. It only takes a moment to collect your things and out you go to the car. The car starts perfectly and you drive away with the music you like to hear playing from your cassette player.

There is quite a bit of traffic building up but there is no delay and you get to work with fifteen minutes to spare. Good, you get your favourite place in the car park. You smile at people you know and greet them cheerfully. You start work in a happy frame of mind.

This attitude continues all day, no matter what challenges arise. You are able to deal with everything without hassle and at the end of the day you feel as though you have achieved a great deal. There is satisfaction about this day and now you are ready to go home, have a meal and do the things you want to do this evening. Altogether a very pleasant day.

WE HAVE FREEDOM OF CHOICE!

We can choose the way our day will turn out by our attitude towards it. If we start off by feeling its not much use trying against all this opposition, then we are lost.

If we choose to recognise that we have power in our lives, we are not puppets, then we are bound to create different circumstances in our world.

It is very important to actively choose to think in a positive way, a good way about ourselves and our environment.

We are here for a purpose, we have lessons to learn which we can only learn right where we are and at this moment in time. We cannot afford to put off until tomorrow what we have to do right now.

So, we start at the beginning of the day, as soon as we wake up. We are determined to choose the right pattern for the day. Remember, what you think and feel at the start of the day sets the pattern in your SCM and then your SCM has no choice but to act on the information you have given it.

YOU HAVE THE CHOICE, your CM your intellect, the thinking part of your mind, can choose to think good, positive things to feed to your SCM. If you use your will power to make sure you stick to a positive programme, then your day will be a great day, filled with opportunities you could never dream of.

A DAILY GOAL:

As I awake:
I give thanks for a peaceful night's sleep.
Then I say, 'Thank you for a new day, a new beginning.'
This is a wonderful, exciting day, filled with opportunities just waiting for me to grasp them!
It's a good day, a great day, what am I going to do with it?

THINGS TO DO!

1. Do not put off anything that you must do today. Make a list at the beginning of the day of all the important things you must do. The most important should head the list. Cross off each item on your list when you have completed it. If you find that despite the fact you have worked diligently through your list you do not have time to do them all, then these items will head your list the next day. This is very important. You may think this is a chore that you can miss out, well if you do then you will really miss out on the results you hope to achieve.

Commitment. Any form of study needs total commitment if any success is to be achieved. No one else can do it for you.

Set a major goal.

This goal should be to make sufficient time each day for study and work with this course. **KEEP AT IT NO MATTER WHAT HAPPENS. Do not be put off by anyone or anything. It will only hamper your progress and you will feel guilty and discouraged.**
Keep encouraging yourself by saying:
"My whole life is changing for the better now."

"I can if I think I can."

"Within me is the creative power of the universe."

"Working with these exercises will uncover talents I have yet to realise."

"I feel healthy, I feel happy, I feel terrific!"

GOAL SETTING.

Once you have decided what your goal is you then have to work out a plan of action for it. This is most important as you cannot just sit back and wait for something to happen. Nothing will happen until you make it happen. Wishing will get you nowhere, but putting your ideas into practice will, and this is how to do it.

FIRST Decide what you want. If your goal is to write a novel then put it down as number one on the long-term goal section on the chart.

SECOND What will you need to do to achieve this? Will you need to enrol for a writing course at the local institute, do you need to buy a typewriter or word processor? This goes down on the medium range goal as number one.

THIRD Your short range goal should now be fairly clear. Every minute of your spare time must be spent in WRITING. So goal one must be to write as much as you can each day.

The rest of the goal chart can be filled in with things that apply to each number one choice.

Deal with the short range goals first as these can make or break your major goal.

Your goal is to write each day. The other four lines can be filled in with what you need to do to enable you to write each day. Can you change things around to give yourself more time, can you delegate something to save time, are you willing to give up certain things, such as TV, nights out, etc. THESE SHORT RANGE GOALS ARE THE MOST IMPORTANT PART OF GOAL SETTING.

If your medium range goal is to take a course of study then your goal could be to apply at the various colleges of instruction for a prospectus. The local library can be very helpful about finding the various courses and tutors.

Whilst there you could also look for 'How to' books on writing.

If you need to buy a typewriter etc then how are you going to buy this? Are you going to work extra hours to earn more money to buy it, are you willing to stop smoking to buy it, are you willing to give up renting videos, buying CDs, records or cassettes? Nights out cost both time and money so you may repeat short and medium goals.

Once these two goals are sorted out then you are well on the way to achieving your major goal, writing a novel. In your long range goals you can include the title, characters and the plot.

The real secret is to plan your novel. Once this plan is firm in your mind and you have sorted out the other goals the rest will follow on in the correct sequence and your novel will be written. You could even give yourself a deadline for finishing it.

Do you see the idea? Short range goals are the things you need to do every day. Medium range follow on from them and cover anything from one to three months or more even. Your long range goal is the ultimate and can take you a few years depending upon many factors in your personal life.

The thing is not to be discouraged and even be prepared to alter the goals whenever this is necessary. Be flexible with everything especially with writing. As you go ahead with your story the characters take over and the finished tale is often different from the one you planned. This is good as it shows you are working from your SCM, your intuition, and this is always highly successful.

Goal setting is an important part of your life. Man is a goal striving animal and is constantly setting goals and achieving them. This is not a new invention it is the normal, natural way we function as human beings. By deliberately setting goals for what you want in your life you counteract the negative goals that we accept unconsciously from the people in our environment. Choose your own goals for only you know what you really need.

SHORT RANGE GOALS

1. _____

2. _____

3. _____

4. _____

5. _____

MEDIUM RANGE GOALS

1. _____

2. _____

3. _____

4. _____

5. _____

LONG RANGE GOALS

1. _____

2. _____

3. _____

4. _____

5. _____

KEY 3. WHO IS DRIVING?

SECTION 3. BAD LUCK.

"It's my bad luck."

"I am jinxed."

"I am never lucky."

Sayings like these are very common among failures.

There is no such thing as luck.

If someone gets promotion, or has a new car, or wins the pools, the majority of people feel envious and say with total belief that the person was lucky.

Again we reiterate, there is no such thing as luck. Nothing happens by chance. We make things happen in our own lives. What we believe about anything will become a reality in our life.

You are a creature of habit. Habit is the function of your SCM. You learned to swim, ride a bicycle, dance, skate and drive a car by consciously doing these things over and over again until they became patterns in your SCM. Then, the automatic habit action of your SCM took over. This is sometimes called second nature which is a reaction of your SCM to your thinking and acting.

You are free to choose a good habit or a bad habit. If you repeat a negative thought or act over a period of time, you will be under the compulsion of a habit. **THE LAW OF YOUR SCM IS COMPULSION.**

You can liken your CM to a camera, and your SCM is the sensitive film on which the picture is registered and impressed.

Films are developed in the dark room, so are mental pictures developed in the darkroom of your SCM.

You must move mentally from the old patterns of thought and in the realm of your own mind dwell on the way you want things to be. If you want to go to London you must first leave Birmingham. Likewise, if you want to be a happy, healthy, prosperous, and highly successful person, you must leave behind you, as a closed book, your old grudges, peeves,

74

criticism of self and others, superstitions, and get a new self image.

Picture yourself the way you want to be not as you are now and this will gradually sink down into your SCM and take root there.

Superstitions are old unrealistic beliefs which we learned in early childhood. When we are very young we are not capable of abstract reasoning so we just accepted what we heard and what we were told by everyone around us. We heard people say, "it's unlucky to do that", and they would promptly do something to counteract the thing that should not have been done.

We are all products of the past thinking of our ancestors. Primitive man realised he was subjected to forces over which he had no control. The sun gave him heat but it also scorched the earth. Fire burned him, thunder terrified him, the water flooded his lands and his cattle were drowned. From his primitive reasoning came a belief in many types of gods. He supplicated himself to the intelligencies of the winds, stars and waters, hoping they would hear him and answer his prayers. He then separated the good guys from the bad guys, the elements which were helpful and those which were not. So from that time we get the superstition of beneficial and malignant powers.

Today we have a hangover from these old superstitious beliefs. God is in heaven surrounded by angels the streets of heaven are paved with gold and if we are good we go there when we die. On the other hand, hell is a bad place somewhere down below and if we are bad we will go down there and be burned in the fire.

Down through the ages theologians have brainwashed and hypnotised people into believing that evil was caused by a devil with hoofs and horns, bat-like ears and a pointed tail, a sort of hideous monster that tempts us to do evil. There is no such being. It is a figment of the imagination and a projection of the distorted twisted imagination of man.

Most people have a belief in two powers, one causing sickness and the other determining the degree of health. They believe that God is punishing them for their past sins, that God has it in for them and they are now reaping their just deserts. All these are false beliefs in the mind.

A woman I know has suffered from severe arthritis for many years. Since she was a child she has been conditioned to a belief that Arthritis was a crippling disease for which there was no cure. Both her mother and grandmother had suffered from this disease and both became incapable of moving about unaided. As a child she had seen the change take place in what appeared to be two healthy adults. This became her firm belief.

I worked with her on this and explained that she was believing in two powers, that one was causing Arthritis and the other was judging her and she decided that she was found wanting.

The cause of all sickness, poverty, misery and suffering in the world *is the belief in them.*

All our suffering, pain and misery is due to our ignorance, misuse and misapplication of universal laws and principles.

There is only one Creative Power, but it is called by many name such as God, Allah, Brahma, Reality, Cosmic Consciousness and many more.

This creative life force, this living Intelligence is throughout the universe. It is everywhere present, in fact, there is no place where it is not found; It is within man himself, It is within **YOU.**

Yes, The Creative life force is within you. As we have said previously, you would not be a living person if there was an absence of this living Intelligence.

This is the Power that you are constantly using, whether you realise it or not.

Once this Arthritic woman realised this, her life changed completely. She began, as I suggested, to meditate upon this Power within herself and ask for guidance. Twice a day she meditated and after a week of this kind of meditation she had a feeling of a Presence that she could talk to. She rang me in an excited state, she said, "What shall I call It?". Again I told her to ask in meditation for a name. She did, and she began to talk to this name within herself and ask questions.

Always she acted on the intuitive feelings that came up from her deeper mind. I gave her advice on diet, exercise and relaxation, which she followed in total belief. She believed because she went within and asked if the advice I gave was right. It was. She improved so much she was able to discontinue the medication and eventually was totally free from pain.

We all have the same Power within us and as we have freedom of choice, we either use it wisely or we misuse it. It is not God punishing us for past wrongdoing, rather we punish ourselves by choosing to believe in two powers. There cannot be two powers, one would cancel out the other and there would be chaos everywhere.

Good and evil are in the mind of the individual!

Whether a thing is good or bad depends upon the use to which it is put. You can use the power of the atom to produce electricity and to drive a submarine or ship across the oceans; or you can destroy cities, towns and people. You can use electricity to illuminate your home; or to kill someone. You can use water to bath a child; or drown it. The same wind that can drive a ship onto the rocks will also carry it to safety.

Do not believe anything that you do not understand.

Every belief tends to manifest itself. If you constantly say negative things about yourself, then these will become a reality in you life.

Your second goal:

Start today to work on a negative habit pattern that you are locked into. First thing in the morning and last thing at night, remember? And as many times as you can catch your-self out. Don't put yourself down. Think about the opposite, the positive, and say it out loud. e.g. "I have always done things this way." change that to, "I am now learning to do things in a new and better way."

Start to change the way you do things. Don't go to and from work exactly the same way, or to the shop or other regular activity. Don't read the same old newspaper all the time. Don't talk the same way. Join a club or go to night school, you can learn something new and meet new people at the same time. See every person from a different viewpoint. We all have the same creative Power within us, so we are all one brotherhood whatever our differences.

KEY 3. WHO IS DRIVING?

All successful men and women possess one outstanding characteristic, that is their ability to make prompt decisions and to persist in carrying those decisions through to completion.

On the other hand, all those who fail have one characteristic in common; they hesitate to make decisions and they vacillate and waver. Also, when they do eventually nake a decision they are not persistent in sticking to the decisions made.

I refuse to make a decision.

A young executive in a class said that he did not know what to do, or what was reasonable or logical in a certain situation, so he would not make a decision about it.

He had already made a decision. He had decided not to make a decision. That meant he had decided to accept whatever came from the mass mind in which we are all immersed. He virtually refused to take charge of his own mind.

After working with this for about three weeks he saw that really he was copping out, not: taking responsibility for his own thinking, reasoning and deduction. That by opting out of decision making he allowed the law of averages, or the mass thinking of the race to make decisions for him. He began working with the following:

"I believe in my inner power which is the creative power of the universe. This creative power within me is all wise, all good and all powerful. All my decisions are based on the fact that this creative power is making all decisions through me, so my decisions must be right."

He learned to make definite decisions about every aspect of his life. He began by having the courage to make a decision even if it seemed to be a wrong one at the time. Nearly always, these so-called wrong decisions proved to be exactly right in the long term. So his confidence grew. Within a year he became manager of a large department within the company and this meant a great salary increase. He enjoyed his work which meant decision making.

You have the capacity to decide.

You are a self-conscious individual and you have the capacity to decide what you want in life. It is wrong to let others decide for you.

You have freedom of choice, that is why you have volition and initiative. This is why you are an individual. Accept your responsibility and make decisions for yourself. Other people do not know best. When you refuse to make decisions for yourself you are actually rejecting the great power and potential within you. You are thinking from the standpoint of the weakness and inferiority of slaves and underlings!

All the power of your SCM is behind your decision. If, for instance, you are a heavy smoker and want to give up smoking, then no amount of will-power will stop you. Your SCM is totally conditioned to the smoking habit, and unless you change the habit pattern in your SCM you will continue to smoke. The power of your SCM is behind your decision to smoke, you programmed it that way and it will not change of of its own accord. You must reverse the decision to smoke.

Try these affirmations:

"I have reached a definite conclusion in my mind that the habit of smoking is obnoxious, unhealthy, disgusting and offensive to myself and other people. My decision is that I want to give up smoking. My powerful SCM supports this decision and I am completely free from this habit. Thank you. It is done."

You personally have the power to direct this wonderful, creative power which is within your SCM. This power is always ready to obey your every thought and belief. It is your obedient servant. It awaits only your use and direction. Your SCM is your most powerful friend. It never sleeps and is constantly reproducing your habitual thinking into form, function, experience and event. Once you get the knack of directing it, you will find it can heal your body, your business, your personal relationships, in fact, every aspect of your life can be changed for the better.

This wonderful, creative power is ready and waiting for you to use it in the same way that the light switch on the wall is waiting to give you light. You can rise up against any obstacle if you want to enough; if you believe you can; and if you use this creative power wisely and constructively.

Many years ago when I was a child and my parents thought I was dying, my mother unknowingly used it. She believed I would get better. She knew the doctor had done all he could and, as she told me many years later, there was only God who could heal me. As she prayed in desperation she felt her prayers were not getting anywhere, so she got out the Bible and found the 23rd Psalm. She read this out loud over and over again. She kept this up all night and just as the day was breaking she felt as if, "those words had gone right inside me." These are her words. She lay down beside me and fell into an exhausted sleep. She said later that she saw me playing with my brothers just as she fell asleep.

I remember waking up and finding my mother fast asleep on the bed with me. I tried to wake her up but my Father came in and told me to let her sleep. He seemed very happy especially when I said I was hungry!

I wondered what all the fuss was about when my Mother eventually woke up. It was a good feeling.

"God works in mysterious ways," said my Mother frequently.

She did not realise just what it was she was doing. She was so desperate that she forced herself to read that Psalm out loud, over and over again until she was exhausted. All that effort went into her SCM and her deeper mind took over and because she believed that God could heal me, It acted upon her belief which became stronger and stronger with every word she read.

She was actually programming her SCM and her SCM responded to her belief.

The Higher Power within us works through our SCM. As you know, your SCM can only react. So whatever we put into it will be produced as a reality.

When I was promoted to Deputy Headmistress I met many problems. My main concern was the students I was teaching. I had a heavy teaching time-table and certain admin duties as well as examinations to contend with.

Certain members of staff were older that I was and rather set in their ways. They did not take kindly to any constructive suggestion I made during staff meetings. In fact, their policy was to block everything I wanted to try. They were very set in their ways and afraid of change. The old way of doing things had worked well for many years so why should a newcomer change things? I knew that I had to get their cooperation or I would never be able to expand the facilities and give the students much needed opportunities for growth and expansion. The most determined of all the staff was the female Head of the English department. She had applied for my post but was turned down, so that was an added niggle for her.

Quite by chance I discovered that we were both married in June on the same day of the month. She was considerably older than I was so it was not the same year. It became a small common ground.

Then, I encouraged the students to use the Library, of which she was in charge, by giving them certain projects to do which meant reference books. She was delighted. No other member of staff ever used the Library nor did they encourage their students to do so; they resented her attitude so they boycotted the school Library and asked students to use the town library.

Most of the older staff had an attitude problem and as a result there was little or no enthusiasm in the school for anything except a tight control on discipline.

I made a point of asking her opinion about certain books and bringing in my own books to show her. We also talked about our families She not only became more cooperative but she defended me staunchly when my suggestions were put forward, and she always agreed to try things out. So, very gently things began to change for the better and when I left the school there were very few dry eyes in the staff-room.

Mentally, I visualised the changes I felt were needed for

the good of the students and I also looked for the good in each one of the staff who were so contentious.

In a nutshell.

1. Make a prompt decision this week to do something. It is another way of setting a goal. If it is a money decision, a health decision, a personal relationship decision, a work decision; whatever you decide, then GO FOR IT. Once the decision is made then carry it through with persistence until it is completed. SEE IT THROUGH!

2. Do not start regretting the decision once it has been made. STICK TO IT. Keep saying over and over, "This is the right decision now. I am giving it to my deeper mind to work on and all is well."

3. Trust your deeper mind. Close your eyes, take a deep breath and relax. As you sit relaxed and at ease, focus your attention on your heart area. Say to your deeper mind in this area, "I trust you completely. No one knows me as you do and you always work to bring the best into my life." As you do this regularly it will become a habit to go within yourself whenever you meet a challenge in your life.

4. Your mind is a powerful tool so use it wisely. Get out of the habit of criticising yourself or anyone else. Your mind will take it up and act upon it to your detriment.

5. Look for the good in everything. If you see or hear an ambulance rushing along, think immediately, "It is going to help someone in need." Do not allow such thoughts as, "There has been an accident." Whatever the situation there is good in it!

From the worst situation a great deal is learned. If you constantly look for the good you will find that your SCM will take over and all your days will be good days!

QUESTIONS.

Q1. Is it advisable to look back to past experiences?

Q2. What do you consider is the main ingredient for success?

Q3. How can you make sure that you have a good day?

Q4. Are we here by chance?

Q5. Why is it important to do things NOW?

Q6. What is a habit?

Q7. Why is our belief so important?

Q8. Does God punish us for our past wrongdoings?

Q9. What old habit pattern have you decided to change?

Q10. What is the outstanding characteristic that all successful people have in common?

Q11. How important is choice?

All the answers are in the sections of the key.

SUNSPOTS

**BEFORE YOU CAN
SOLVE A PROBLEM. YOU
MUST FIRST
UNDERSTAND IT!**

KEY 4. WHAT DO I SEE?

Every teacher knows the tremendous value of Visual Aids. If a visual image is presented to children they learn much more quickly than if they just listened to an explanation. Talk and chalk went out years ago. The value of pictures and models etc stimulates the mind and enhances the learning capacity.

Local Education Authorities allow Art Galleries to exhibit paintings in schools. Children are exposed to art of all kinds on the walls of the corridors of their school. Periodically these are changed so there is always a fresh stimulus of something new to be seen. How many children would ever go to an Art Gallery if left to their own devices? This way they assimilate new experiences in their environment that stimulate interest, particularly if the Art teacher uses this wisely.

Pictures are very important. In fact, every picture tells a story. But what that story is all about depends upon the person viewing the picture. What one person can see in a picture another person cannot. We all see from our own standpoint, from our own level of development.

A child would not see the same significance in a picture as a mature adult would. The mature mind looks for sophistication whilst the child sees only simplicity.

We also see what we want to see. Unpleasantness is glossed over so that only half-truth is observed. Also our memories of past events colour our attitude towards pictures of any kind.

Do we see things as they really are?

Why are pictures important?

"As a man thinketh in his heart, so is he."

You are constantly thinking, you never stop. You do not think in words, you think in pictures. This is how your mind works. Your mind is constantly creating pictures and this is done through your imagination.

People frequently say, "It's your imagination." What they mean is, you are making a mountain out of a molehill, you are exagerating, they do not believe what you say. In other words, your imagination is something you need to curb, or to forget.

Your imagination is the most wonderful, the most powerful tool you have, it is not something to be ashamed of but something to cherish, to be grateful for. It is your most valuable asset. This mind power of imagination can change your life, if you will let it. You need to learn how to use it wisely. Let's do a little exercise.

What did you have for breakfast this morning? Think about this, let your imagination fill in all the details. Smell the toast, crunch it. Smell the aroma of the coffee, was it black or white? Or, did you have tea? What about cereal or bacon and eggs? Use your senses, smell, taste, touch, feel, hear all the things you had for breakfast.

You saw all this as pictures. You did not see the written words, toast, eggs, coffee etc. Your mind faithfully produces the pictures of the happenings of the day. The thoughts we have are pictures in our mind and when these pictures combine with corresponding feelings, they become a reality in our life. It is a Universal Law—you cannot think one thing and expect another.

"As a man thinketh in his heart means, we think with our intellect, our CM but the corresponding feeling is the emotion felt by the thought. This is from the SCM which is the emotional area.

Your thoughts make you what you are. You cannot think poor and expect to be rich; you cannot think sickness and expect health.

Do you remember the imagination exercise "Start the day right?" Each time we think we have a corresponding feeling and this goes into our SCM where it grows and develops. If it is a negative thought there is a negative feeling which your ever active SCM takes hold of and works with, to your detriment. If the thought is a good, constructive one then that is what your SCM will produce.

You sow the seeds (thoughts) and these germinate in the

rich, fertile soil of your SCM which faithfully produces exactly what you have sown. In your garden if you want tomatoes you will sow tomato seeds, you will not sow cabbage seeds. You reap what you sow. Each thought produces after its own kind. So good produces good in your life and bad produces bad in your life. This is a proven fact.

ANOTHER POINT TO REMEMBER. We do not think isolated thoughts. One thought leads to another.One thought suggests a related thought which suggests a thought related to it...and so on. Your thoughts are mental pictures and mental pictures in a continuous sequence are mental videos. These mental videos—projected intensely and repeatedly on the mental video screen of your SCM—are materialised into reality in your life.

Someone has said, "People have a self-image and become what they envision (mentally picture) themselves to be." This is quite true. Many students constantly play the mental video of themselves failing at something. They relive, in all the tiniest detail, every aspect of that failure. The more they play this video the more powerful it becomes. By constant repetition they are very firmly fixing this failure video in their mind and the SCM has no choice but to accept it and faithfully reproduce it in their lives. Consequently they are failures at everything they try. Your mental pictures determine your future because;

They guide you to;
and attract to you,
the opportunities,
the personal contacts,
the financial and other means
YOU need
to reach YOUR goal in life!

What you physically see is one way in which mental pictures are formed and impressed on your SCM. **The rich get richer.** Rich people constantly see the wealth that surrounds them, so their mental pictures are of wealth. **They think rich** because they mentally picture what they see.

The poor get poorer The poor constantly see the

poverty which surrounds them so their mental pictures are of poverty. They mentally picture what they physically see, so, **The poor get poorer.**

Universal law of Consistency.

The law of Cosistency requires that what you plant—to be consistent—must produce a harvest of only what you plant.

These pictures produced by your surroundings need not be dominant.

You can deliberately produce much more powerful, dominant, vital controlled mental pictures by the use of your Imagination.

Because you can produce mental pictures deliberately **you can control your mental pictures.**

You can imagine whatever mental pictures you CHOOSE -to imagine, If you consistently imagine wealth, success, health, good personal relationships or whatever it is you want, then your SCM will work to bring this to you.

IMPORTANT

Your mental pictures **Guide** you to the reality of whatever you—consistently, repeatedly, intensely—mentally picture. Please note that your SCM guides you. *You have to follow that guidance.* You cannot be guided if you do not respond. You cannot just sit back and wait for something to happen like a bolt out of the blue. It doesn't work like that.

Inner guidance is received in many ways.

You could pick up a newspaper and read something, someone could say something, you could be guided to buy a book or magazine from which an idea will seem to stand out from the rest. You could overhear a conversation, or see something on TV.

Whatever you learn from this course MUST be put into practice.

You have to DO IT!

The power to achieve is generated by DOING; You generate NO power by NOT DOING. As you do—you will receive. **So do this,** use your imagination to keep your mind filled with controlled mental pictures of whatever you want.

USE YOUR IMAGINATION!

KEY 4. WHAT DO I SEE

SECTION 2. TAKE DOWN THE DUDS.

What kind of pictures are hanging on the wall of your mind? Are there old, old pictures of injury, insult, resentment unhappiness? Do these dusty old pictures keep reminding you of old hurts that should have been removed long ago.

Well now is the time to do something about it. You are going to take down the duds because you have no use for them in your life. They are taking up valuable space which could be occupied by fresh, new talents and ideas.

Spring cleaning.

We will use our creative imagination to clean out the old attic, your mind, of stuff that is quite useless to you.

Imagine yourself going upstairs to the attic. You slowly open the door and are faced with darkness. Slowly, carefully, you feel your way towards where you think the light switch should be.

You find it and switch on, but nothing happens. You realise that the bulb must have either been removed or broken, so very gingerly you feel your way towards the window. The attic is full of all kinds of stuff, old furniture, boxes, all kinds of things are in your way as you slowly and carefully move towards the window. After knocking yourself several times and coughing because of the dust you are disturbing, you finally make the window. What a relief to pull back the dusty old curtains. The old sash window is stiff but you manage to pull it up and you gratefully gulp in the fresh air. Looking round at the room you are amazed at the rubbish left up there for so many years. Broken toys, bring back memories of days long gone. You take time to wander around recalling old times, good and bad. You stay like this for a time. Suddenly you have a great urge to clear the lot out and you start with a will to remove as much as you can. Time means nothing to you as you work. Your aim is to clear out as much as you can.

Soon the room is cleared. Old, broken furniture is taken outside ready for burning. Old newspapers, magazines are stacked for the bonfire. Everything has to go, you have no further use for any of it.

The attic looks different now. The old curtains are torn down, the walls have been swept and the floor scrubbed. It is a clean, open attic, ready for something of value to be placed there, something to be seen and enjoyed not hidden away.

You feel exhilarated as you look round the now bare room and you begin to plan how you will use it and what you will put into it.

This room is going to be a very special room. It will be totally yours, no one else will have access to it. So you now plan the colour scheme. You imagine very clearly the walls, paintwork and curtains hanging at the window. The furniture and the carpeting are as clear in your mind as if they were already in there. Now, what kind of pictures are you going to hang on the walls? They must be ones that you really like and enjoy looking at, pictures that mean something to you. Do you have flowers and plants in your room?

This is your very special room. Anytime you feel restless, unhappy or depressed, make an effort to sit down for a while in a chair and close your eyes and gently build up the picture of your own special room. Imagine yourself actually in the room, sitting down in one of the comfortable chairs and looking at your favourite pictures. In this room, this private place, you will regain your composure and you will rise from the chair, walk to the door, take a last look around then go through the door and close it behind you. You will then open your eyes and return to your everyday matters.

This simple exercise of the imagination will, if done regularly, give you a means of escape from the temporary hassles of the day.

We mentioned previously that you can deliberately control your mental pictures. In fact, all the exercises using your imagination are helping you to do just that. The more intensely you project them on to your mental screen, your SCM, the more they will become your life-guidance system.

You become whatever you repeatedly, intensely mentally picture what you will be—for better or for worse—depending on the kind of mental picture you project into you SCM.

For better or for worse! If you do not control your mental video then uncontrolled thoughts (mental pictures) will find all the mental spaces not filled with your controlled thoughts.

These uncontrolled thought pictures may be pleasant day dreams, but more often than not they are mental picture situations of all the worries, anxieties, fears, resentments, hatreds or guilt complexes which have been suppressed in your SCM. Your SCM always takes the first opportunity to feed back these into your conscious mind.

This repeats and reinforces NEGATIVE thought pictures which become your life-guidance system, with disastrous results.

WHATEVER IS SUPPRESSED IN YOUR SCM IS UNDESIRABLE—IT WOULD NOT BE SUPPRESSED IF IT WERE DESIRABLE

So we need a way of turning off negative and undesirable mental pictures.

Here is a way.

We are now going to discuss the various ways of achieving a QUIET mind.

1. As you settle down in your chair and close your eyes, just let go of your body. Imagine it to be heavy and you simply let it go. You let the chair take the strain. You have no need to think about your body at all now. Take a few deep breaths and then settle down to normal breathing.

2. Now your body is out of the way we turn to your mind. You do not have to think about anything at this time. If negative thoughts try to come in, just mentally say, "I have no use for you in my life at this moment." and immediately think BLACK.

3. Think of your mind being filled with TOTAL

BLACKNESS. BLACK. No mental pictures of disturbing situations. NO MENTAL PICTURES OF ANYKIND! Black out all mental pictures so that your mind is filled with deep darkness, BLACK. In this blackout there is no room for any mental pictures. Actively mainta:in this total mental blackout until your mind is relaxed and quiet.

4. Once you have achieved a quiet mind you can then, calmly and deliberately replace the temporary darkness with bright intense, controlled mental pictures of what you want.

A quiet mind—undisturbed by any mental pictures—is a mind at PEACE

This is the aim of this exercise and remember, practice makes perfect.

You can, if you prefer, THINK GREY instead of black. Grey is a softer colour, but it must be opaque, it must fill your mind. It must totally block out all mental pictures. You can also imagine heavy fog filling your mind. If you imagine heavy fog, it has the advantage of sustaining your interest in the OBSCURING material. This will keep your mind from mental pictures you do not want. Begin by filling your mind with wisps of fog which you mentally turn into thicker, fluffy clouds, and then into dense fog which totally obscures all mental pictures. Your mind is completely filled with dense, impenetrable FOG—and NO MENTAL PICTURES.

You can also use other dark colours, midnight blue or very deep purple. The colour must be opaque enough to totally obscure mental pictures.

Do not use any bright colour e.g. red, yellow, orange, or any bright shade of any colour.

The objective is complete mental relaxation while you entirely obscure all mental pictures by filling your mind with a neutral, pleasant, opaque colour or substance (fog) which no mental pictures can penetrate.

Do not give up this exercise because you feel you cannot sustain the opaque mind for long.

By constant repetition your SCM will take up this idea and then you will be able to do it whenever you want to do it. It will seem perfectly natural for you to automatically do this.

When you try the exercise, praise yourself! even if you feel you have not been as successful at it as you would like to be.

Your SCM loves praise and you deserve it anyway for working at the exercise.

Eventually, the benefits you will reap from this exercise, will be enormous. As you blank out your mind you are allowing yourself to relax completely. This has a wonderfully, beneficial effect on your whole body, particularly your internal organs and your eyes. If you have eye problems of any kind this exercise can be used with visualisation and eye exercises which promote clearer sight. I personally use this every day for the benefit of my eyes.

I sit in a comfortable chair with my eyes closed and I palm my eyes. I cup my eyes with my hands and think total blackness. I keep this up for as long as I want too. I also do exercises whilst my eyes are cupped like this.

Keeping my eyes closed all the time I look up to the top of my vision, then down to the bottom of my vision three times each. Then I think total blackness. I go on to move my closed eyes sideways then rest into total blackness. All the time my hands are cupping my eyes. I continue with the exercises by going from upper right to lower left three times then reverse it upper left and lower right. Finally I lift my closed eyes to the top of my vision then move my eyes clockwise round three times then anti-clockwise. Alway pause between each exercise and visualise total blackness This takes a few minutes to do but the benefits are tremendous. The warmth from the palms of your hands help the eye muscles to relax and by visualising blackness between each exercise you do not allow extraneous thoughts to come in and spoil the relaxation.

Try it anyway.

Our eye muscles are affected by our emotions, so tight thoughts mean tight eye muscles. Relaxed thoughts mean relaxed eye muscles.

KEY 4. WHAT DO I SEE?

SECTION 3. MAKE 'EM REAL!

Your SCM is lierally bombarded with countless stimulation from your five senses, your thoughts, impulses, memory recalls and responses; in addition to the very complex operation of your physical and mental life functions. Most of these take place below or beyond your level of consciousness. You are quite unaware that all this is going on.

Your SCM is obviously very engrossed with all this and added to this is the enormous pressure of unexpected and sudden challenges which occur daily.

So in view of all this, you cannot expect your SCM to take very much notice of a vague, not very clear, mental picture of your goal. Especially if you only picture it when you remember; or you feel unsure of what it is you really want from life.

You cannot expect your SCM to disregard the enormous pressures upon it, and to give top priority to an indifferent, infrequent, indistinct mental picture of your goal. Certainly not!

Your SCM WILL USE ITS UNLIMITED POWER TO GUIDE YOU TO—OR ATTRACT TO YOU WHATEVER YOU WANT, IN DIRECT PROPORTION TO THE INTENSITY AND FREQUENCY OF YOUR MENTAL PICTURES.

Many years ago I trained for the theatre and I remember one young actor telling me about his desire. He loved acting at school and played many parts. His father wanted him to carry on the family business when he left school. This young man had a yearning to act, in fact to be a famous actor. His parents were totally against this. He never talked about acting to them but he would constantly daydream about acting. He used to make his mental picture so real he could actually see himself acting on a London stage. He went through all the parts he had ever played and imagined famous actors with him on stage. He finally left home to follow his dream.

He got a job in a hotel, and spent his spare time going to

as many theatres as he could afford on his poor pay. Always he kept up his daydreams and actually would write his own name on the many programmes he collected. He vividly pictured himself playing the parts.

He eventually got a job in the theatre as ASM with small acting parts. A strange twist to the story. He found that once he actually had the opportunity to act, the real, burning desire for it left him and he became very interested in directing. He spent some years as a very successful director then he found that directing was not what he wanted. His real desire came when he was in his thirties. He wanted to teach. So he started again with, as he put it, my daydreams.

We met when we were together at a Conference and over ten years had elapsed since he was directing in the theatre.

"It took all those years of daydreaming and achieving my goals for me to realise where my talents really lay."

He is still a very successful teacher and all the experiences he had throughout his young life are used to great advantage in what he is now doing.

YOUR DEEPER MIND WILL ALWAYS SHOW YOU THE WAY, BUT BE PREPARED TO CHANGE THINGS. YOUR SCM KNOWS YOUR TALENTS AND—EVENTUALLY YOU FIND THEM THROUGH MANY EXPERIENCES.

Real pictures.

Your pictures must be as real as you can make them. You not only see them very clearly but you feel them also. Put enthusiasm into the pictures. Act as if you already have what it is you want. In fact, imagine you are an actor playing a role. You are the star of your mental video. See yourself confidently doing what it is you want to do, having what it is you want to have. This will put life into your picture and give your SCM something to work on.

Success means successful living. So let us work now on three steps to success.

First Step. Find the thing you love to do, then DO IT!
Success is in loving your work. If you love your work you

will do it with all your whole self. You will not see it as a means of passing time. You will not see it as a chore, something which has to be done for you to earn money.

It will be a labour of love to which you dedicate yourself wholeheartedly. The reward will be in a wonderful sense of achievement, a satisfaction of a job well done. Loving what you do will motivate you to find out all you can about the job; go on courses of study; bring out new ideas etc.

My life goal was to be a teacher. There was no way I could ever achieve this. At thirty seven I went to college. There was a way, I only had to tune in to my SCM and my Deeper Mind (SPCM—Super conscious mind) guided me to all the things I needed to start. It was wonderful. I loved my work and each holiday I went on a course of study which kept me in touch with new educational developments and broadened my own outlook considerably.

My affirmation then was, "The Infinite Intelligence of my SCM reveals to me my true place in life."

I repeated this lovingly, quietly and positively to my Deeper Mind every night just as I was in a drowsy state before going to sleep. It became a kind of gentle lullaby which I mentally spoke within. In the drowsy state before sleep you are at the Alpha level of consciousness where you contact your SCM. So the input then is very powerful.

If you do this gently over a period of time you will have great results. I know, I did it and I still do it!

Second Step. Stick to one kind of work and become an expert in that field.

This step ties up with the first step. I specialised in people rather than subjects and so I was guided to administration. The first step was to become Head of a department after only two years teaching. I learned all I could about that subject and kept up with the new thought. I was also learning to deal with people, two years later I became deputy head and finally head of a secondary school.

This did not just happen out of the blue. I found myself doing things I had never dreamed I could do and, like my actor friend, I used my imagination to see the end result of my desire.

It never ceases to amaze me how wonderful the mind is.

Third Step. This is most important. You must be quite sure that the thing you want to do is not just for your own benefit, it must also benefit others in some way. Your desire must not be selfish, it must benefit humanity. If your motive is only to benefit yourself then this is not a complete circuit, there is a short circuit and you experience some lack or limitation, or sickness.

In other words, your motive should be to help humanity by serving.

We all know people who are totally selfish and become very wealthy by cheating others. On the surface they appear to be highly successful if you judge from the outer appearance. When we cheat, lie, steal from another we are actually robbing ourselves. Our Deeper mind (SPCM) knows what we do and acts upon the feelings and motives within. We cannot fool our SPCM so we find people who do cheat etc often lose their wealth, their families, their health in fact everything. We cannot judge by appearances.

What we think and feel we create. We create what we believe. A person who accummulates a fortune by fraudulent means is not successful. There is no success without peace of mind and what good is a massive fortune if the person cannot sleep at night, is sick, or has a guilt complex?

Many scientists and businessmen use a simple technique for success. They quietly say the abstract term "success" over and over, inplanting it into their SCM until they reach a conviction that SUCCESS IS THEIRS. They know that the idea of success contains all the esential elements of success. If you do this and repeat "success" over and over with faith and conviction your SCM will eventually accept it as true.

Use your imagination. Make a habit of going to sleep every night feeling successful. Believe you were born to succeed; YOU WERE!

Make your pictures real. Act as if you are already success-ful. See yourself as confidently doing the thing you really want to do.

If your goal is clear and definite then your SCM will guide you to the things, people or circumstances you need to get started. Never give in to negative thoughts or pictures in your mind. Bring them out and examine them for what they are, NOTHING TRYING TO BE SOMETHING. They are without substance and are fed by fear.

Your thoughts fused with feeling become your beliefs and according to your belief is it done to you!

The power of sustained imagination draws forth the miracle working powers of your SCM.

YOU WERE BORN TO SUCCEED.

KEY 4. WHAT DO I SEE?

SECTION 4. CUT IT OUT!

This section deals with practical ways in which you can stimulate your SCM.

You can create anything you imagine. The only limitation is in the negative use of your imagination. If there is failure and lack in your life it is because you first imagined it in your mind. It is likewise in mind that you can begin dissolving those limatations and remaking your life into what you want it to be.

The imagination is a much stronger force than will power; and when the imagination and will are in conflict the imagination always wins. Often when a mental picture is first suggested, the will does not want to accept that picture. But when the mental picture is repeated sufficiently, the SCM has no choice but to accept it and to bring it to pass, no matter how unlikely the mental picture appears to the reasoning power of the will.

Since you are hoping for greater good in your life, you should begin to form the mental image of it in your mind. Your reasoning power may tell you that it can never be, but that doesn't matter.

Your will may say that your dream is too big to come true, that it is impossible to fulfil. But, if you just dare to continue imaging it anyway, then your imagination will go to work for you to produce the visible result you have been imaging, and in due time your will can also work for you. Whatever the mind is taught to expect, it will build, produce and bring into being for you.

Sometimes the imaging power of the mind produces immediate results, but if it takes longer, you can rest assured that when the results do come they will be bigger and better than you ever imagined.

Throughout history people have used their creative imagination to bring about what they desired.

As I said previously, visual aids are a good way of helping to reinforce your mental pictures.

Napoleon used a large wall map with coloured flags indicating the various moves he planned for his army to nake, months in advance. He also wrote down his desires and plans so as to clarify them and start them into action from the invisible. These techniques were highly successful but his downfall came when he used these same techniques in a destructive way.

Treasure Map.

Take a large sheet of lightweight card, it can be as big as you want it to be, and print the words **Treasure Map** in large letters at the top.

Divide it into four sections with a heading on each section. These sections are the areas of your life that you want to change or improve in some way.

HEALTH, WEALTH, WORK OR BUSINESS, HOLIDAY, MARRIAGE, HOUSE, CAR, whatever it is you want in your life right now.

When you have chosen your headings collect as many magazines, photographs, newspaper cuttings, picture postcards etc that you can find and choose the pictures that correspond with your desire.

e.g. If it is a new car you want then decide which make and model of car you desire. Go to a car showroom. See the car. Is it the colour you want Sit in it to get the feel of the steering wheel and the controls. Touch the upholstery, smell it, make the picture in your mind as vivid as you can. Talk to the salesman, ask for a colour brochure. Be as confident as you can when you talk to him.

One of our students, a music student of twenty two, needed a car to get to college as the train and bus fares were more than he could manage. His friends urged him to buy an old 'banger' but he refused as he wanted a reliable car. He made his treasure map and stuck coloured pictures of the make and model of car he wanted. It was interesting to see his map. He wanted a new car. It was the latest small car on the market with many extras. Fellow students in the class felt he was being too ambitious in his circumstances, they judged by appearances, but he was insistant.

The first thing that happened was, his tutor aked him if he would like to coach his friend's son who had just bought a guitar. He did and this led to the boy bringing his friends along also. He had a small class of keen young boys which gave him a great deal of satisfaction and also money.

The next thing he noticed was that he was making economies which he had never thought would be possible.

He then went to see his bank manager. This man worked out a plan of repayment that was in keeping with his grant and earnings.

He went to the salesroom and explained that he could get the finance but he did not have quite enough money for the deposit. The salesman took him to the back of the showroom and there was the exact car he wanted and had dreamed about. It was secondhand but looked new. The previous owner had bought it for his wife who used it for three months then decided she wanted a shooting brake to put the kids and the animals in together.

It was in perfect condition and at a much lower price. He not only afforded the deposit, but his bank manager was pleased he did not need the full loan.

"It works!" he said joyfully.

He thought big despite the opinions of friends. He did not compromise his dream!

Fill in the other sections with whatever you want at this moment. If one section is for a holiday then go to a travel agent and collect as many brochures of the country you want to visit. Be very specific about the places you want to go to. Cut out the various pictures of hotels, resorts, the airline etc, anything to give your SCM something to work on.

Fill in the other sections and then hang it on a wall or somewhere you can see it constantly.

Scrap book.

Some students prefer to make a scrap book instead of a wall chart. That's fine, especially if you do not wish anyone else to see it. You must however make time each day to look through your scrap book and feel the reality of each picture. Know that this is what is going to happen. Believe in it.

You can also make a quicky scrap book or wall chart.

You simply have one goal only, a car, holiday, money etc. Your mind then has only one subject to work on and can give full attention to it. The results will appear more quickly.

One student who needed money made a wheel of fotune out of a piece of green card. She cut out a large wheel and on it placed some play money her children used in a game. She used only large notes, she was thinking big, and she made out a cheque to herself for a very large amount. Three times a day she would get out her wheel of fortune, which she hid in her wardrobe, and she would study these notes and cheque. At the same time she 'saw' these notes bulging in her purse and herself receiving this large cheque through the post.

She kept this up for over three months; she felt she wanted to make sure her SCM took hold of the idea of a lot of money. It worked! She never again had an empty purse, there was always money enough to buy what she wanted. The final thing astounded her. Out of the blue she received a letter from the solicitor of an aunt who had died recently. This lady was not her real aunt, she had been a friend of her mother. The solicitor stated that £10,000 was for the happy little girl who gave me so much joy. This lady had been her mother's school friend who was unable to have children herself. Until the student was about fourteen years of age she had spent a lot of time with this aunt during school holidays. The aunt went abroad to live and after a while correspondence ceased. She did not know that the aunt had moved back to England neither did she know she had died. It was quite a shock, particularly when she showed us the cheque she had written out to herself. It was for £10,000!

She said, "All I was doing was making sure my SCM got the message,"

Well it certainly did, and other students began to realise that they cannot force anything to happen. All they could do was to set the scene and work at it constantly, even when they felt it was not working.

In other words, **BELIEVE IT!**

Image what you really want, not what you think you can probably have. **Do not compromise.** The image makes the conditions, but it is up to you to make the image. So there is no need to try and force anything. Just gently but clearly image what you want in your life right now and then trust your SCM to do the rest.

Image the best for yourself, you deserve it. You are worth it.

Also, image the best for other people

P.S. GREEN AND GOLD ARE PROSPERITY COLOURS!

QUESTIONS

Q1. Why are pictures important?

Q2. How can you achieve complete mental relaxation?

Q3. What is meant by 'real pictures?

Q4. Why is it important to lull yourself to sleep feeling successful?

Q5. Why is it important not to compromise?

IT IS VERY IMPORTANT THAT YOU MAKE A VISUAL AID.

CHOOSE EITHER A WALL CHART, A SCRAP BOOK, OR A WHEEL OF FORTUNE.

IT IS VERY IMPORTANT THAT YOU LOOK AT YOUR VISUAL AID AS MANY TIMES A DAY AS YOU CAN. AT LEAST TWICE A DAY, MORE IF YOU CAN. REMEMBER, YOU MUST MAKE THE TIME TO DO THESE THINGS, YOU CANNOT WAIT UNTIL YOU HAVE TIME!

SUNSPOTS

"What you can do, or
dream you can, begin it.
Boldness has genius,
power and magic in it."
GOETHE

KEY 5. WATCH YOUR WORDS.

SECTION 1. WHAT DID I SAY?

As a child you no doubt remember your mother or teacher saying to you, "What did I say?" You had to repeat the words that had been said to you. Oh, the anxiety of trying to remember the exact words that were spoken, for you knew if you did not say them correctly you would be in trouble.

The adult who said this to you wanted to be sure you understood exactly what was said. By making you repeat it, it would be more firmly established in your mind.

So from early childhood you were made to repeat words after an adult. As a baby you did this willingly, you imitated the sounds made by your mother and the adults around you without understanding what they meant. You wanted to be one of them. You wanted to do everything they did. You wanted to learn about life. You loved it.

You experienced the power of having someone rush to do your bidding. You wanted more. You commanded at the top of your voice when you were hungry, wet or hurt, knowing there was somebody who would rush to your aid. You yelled and screamed for attention and you cooed and gurgled with delight when you were pleased.

The power of command was very strong then and it was necessary for your survival.

As you grew older, you were taught not to be so demanding and you gradually learned to depend upon yourself for the things you needed.

Unfortunately most adults have lost the power of command. Assertion for what one feels are one's rights has somehow faded into an attitude of 'anything for a quiet life.' Now is the time to start taking command of your life.

The word "command" means to have authority or take control.

Through an attitude of authority you can take control of the good you wish to experience in your life.

Many people look "up" at life, as though it is a mountain towering way above them. They feel insignificant. The law of command helps you to move up to the summit and look out over your world with a feeling of authority and control, which then produces results.

Command.

A positive assertion of the good you wish to experience is often all that is needed to turn the tide of events to produce good for you speedily and easily. It is amazing how quickly doors will open up to you when you dare to take control of a situation and command your high expectations to manifest themselves.

Thou shalt decree a thing and it shall be established unto thee and light shall shine upon thy ways.

Job 22:28

This means that when you command or decree something you want in your life: having set goals, made lists, and mentally and physically pictured it, then it will appear. You will also have a greater understanding of what the laws of life are all about.

You are constantly making decrees, so you are using the law of command every day. Very often they are the wrong kind of decrees which produce what you do not want in your life.

Students of the mind have always been taught the power of words. The spiritual leaders of China, Egypt, India, Persia and Tibet, taught their students to speak only when they had something constructive to say. Because they knew the danger of idle talk they set up a standard to determine whether it was wise to say a thing or not.

1. Is it true?
2. Is it kind?
3. Is it needful?

Even if it is true, if it is not kind, then surely it is not needful!

Today we don't use the word command. People talk about 'affirmations'. Thousands of people all over the world are using and proving that the daily practice of the use of verbal and silent affirmations is the simplest way of using the law of command to obtain good in their lives.

It is such a simple way of bringing about good results that people cannot believe it at first. They expect something very complicated.

Never underestimate the power of words. You make your world with your words.

Jehovah created the earth by commanding...**Let there be...and there was!**

If you do not like the world you have built up with words of discord, lack, limitation, hard times, sickness, poor relationships, then you can change it! Start to build a new world of limitless good, prosperity, health, happiness and contentment.

The **Law of command** is one of the easiest and fastest ways of producing rich results.

What you say about anything is your firm belief. You believe it wholeheartedly or you would not say it. We believe many things that are not true, things which were said to us as children by people around us and which we accepted as true because we did not know any better. Things said jokingly about yourself or others are accepted by your SCM because your SCM is a servant which obeys your instructions.

WORDS ARE POWERFUL.

Words, particularly vowel sounds, set up a vibration which is taken up by your SCM and worked on. Everything in the universe is vibratory even though it appears to be solid. Any scientist will tell you this elementary fact or law of physics. This is the nature of the universe and it is our nature. Words vibrate on the various nerve centres of the body and either create or destroy body cells.

So we must **watch what we say** from now on.

You must use definite words of command for definite needs. For instance, if your money supply is low or your purse is empty, take it in your hands and privately affirm out loud, **THANK YOU FOR THE RICHES OF THE**

UNIVERSE WHICH ARE NOW BEING DEMONSTRATED IN YOU AND THROUGH YOU.

I SEE YOU FILLED TO OVERFLOWING WITH GREAT ABUNDANCE NOW.

Words are powerful particularly words of praise and thanks. Saying thank you means you are recognising and appreciating something or someone. People always respond to thanks and praise, so it is in our own best interest to do this as often as we can.

When you have a meal praise the effort that has gone into the preparation and cooking of it. Give thanks for all the food you eat, remembering that there are others not so fortunate. Praise and appreciate your clothes also.

Take affirmative statements which meet your particular needs and declare them over and over verbally for at least 15 minutes each day. You can split the time up into 3 five-minute periods if that is more convenient. If one of your periods is when you are near people and cannot say them out loud, write them down 15 times, or as many times as you feel you need to.

Writing things down is also powerful. You are making a brain cell impression, and you actually have this written down to look at whenever you need to. Remember how the teacher made you write out things maybe a hundred times? She had the right idea.

Stick affirmations throughout the house where you can see them.

I can if I think I can! is a good reminder to stick on your desk, writing place, dashboard of the car etc.

I give thanks for ever increasing health, youth and beauty. is a great affirmation to stick on your make up mirror or bathroom mirror. Men can alter the words slightly.

My words are charged with prospering power! This is good to say at the start of the day. Then go on to give thanks for a new day, a new beginning.

I give thanks that every day, in every way, I am growing richer and richer in health, wealth and understanding.

110

KEY 5. WATCH YOUR WORDS.

SECTION 2. MATCH WORDS WITH PICTURES.

A group of sixth-form students who were studying history with me asked how they could stop freezing up at exams. We worked out an affirmation;

My wonderful SCM knows all the answers. I am letting the power of my SCM work through me. I know, I remember, I understand. I express myself perfectly.

With the affirmation I told them to see themselves sitting the examination and writing the answers to the questions with enthusiasm. I told them to make the pictures real and to actually feel themselves in the room with the invigilator walking round.

At first some of them had difficulty making the mental pictures real, because memories of past examination failure kept coming into their minds.

We went into the large hall where exams were usually taken which I had already laid out with desks and chairs in exam style. They took their places as they would for the actual exam.

I spoke to them as an invigilator and gave out past history papers to each student. Then for one hour we went through the procedure of answering some of the questions.

I did this each night after school for four weeks before the exam. After each mock sitting they were told to imagine the experience when they were in bed and just about to go to sleep After one week they all felt much better and more confident about taking the examination. They made sure the affirmation was said as many times as possible and frequently I could hear them saying it out loud together as I entered the classroom for the session. I joined in with them, we made it a game, but the words were a command and the picture was firm.

The pictures must match the words. If they don't then confusion arises in your mind. Your SCM needs clear, firm pictures together with clear, firm statements or commands.

The students made their mental pictures real and clear by actually acting as if they were in the examination room. They felt themselves sitting in the hall, being given papers by an invigilator, by writing the answers to history papers. Their visualisations were as near perfect as they could get them. Their command, firm affirmation, was spoken with authority and conviction. The two together worked wonders. Each student had a very high grade pass.

You must be willing to pay the price for success, daily affirmation and visualisation. There is no easier or more interesting way of changing your thinking.

YOU BECOME WHAT YOU WANT TO BE BY AFFIRMING THAT YOU ALREADY ARE.

EASY DOES IT!

The real key to successfully affirming and visualising is to take it easy. By that I mean there should be no anxiety, no strain, no trying hard to achieve your goal. We tend to try hard by the conscious use of our will-power, by straining and worrying and even talking about and picturing all the things that could possibly go wrong. Do you see what you are doing by worrying and focusing the attention on the wrong things? You are giving attention, therefore power, to the very things you do not want in your life.

Your spoken words are powerful so make sure that you are saying good, positive constructive things, things you want in your life rather than what could go wrong. A lot of people seem to think that if they voice their fear thoughts then the things feared will not happen! They do not understand that the things they fear will come about because they are thinking, picturing and talking about them.

By using affirmations you are deliberately building up a constructive idea in your consciousness. Over the years your consciousness has become jammed full with destructive ideas, negative thought-forms. As you now continually affirm positive, constructive ideas about yourself and your affairs, you will slowly but surely dilute and dissolve the destructive, negative habits.

Words are very powerful. In fact words and thoughts are a form of radio activity. As like attracts like it is essential to keep our words constructive to allow the building up of new cells in the body and also to attract the good things of life to us.

Many people say, "I am in a rut." They know what is wrong but they do not understand how they got there and what they can do about it. To get out of a rut they need a new idea to work on. But new ideas are stifled if our consciousness is filled with negativity.

A new idea will generate enthusiasm and even more ideas will come as you work consistently. To be successful at anything you need enthusiasm. If you are a salesman you need enthusiasm for the products you are selling. Whatever work you do you need enthusiasm. A person with enthusiasm is an interesting one, someone who attracts friends, opportunities and success.

The imaging faculty of our mind, our imagination, is the creative faculty We must be very careful to choose words which bring a flash of the completion of our goal. For instance, a student came with an empty purse to a class and said she had no money. She opened her purse and turned it upside down saying, "It's completely empty." She had no money left for the rest of the week for bus fares. We were alone at the time so we started affirming, **I see this purse crammed with money, it is packed with five pound notes, ten pound notes, twenty pound notes, fifty pound notes, and bulging with coins. It is filled to capacity.** We laughed a lot as we were doing this and she suddenly said that her purse seemed to feel heavy. We stopped at that and students began to arrive.

The class filled up and just as we were about to start in rushed a late student. He sat down by the young student with the empty purse. He began talking excitedly to her then pulled out a £5.00 note and gave it to her. We were all enthralled by this interchange and we were curious. This is what he said:

"I had been working on my money consciousness this last two weeks, but instead of realising money I could not spin out the money I had. It seemed as though I was going from bad to worse. I kept on affirming, what else could I do? I refused to let the fact that I was short of money discourage me. I kept on and on, especially when I could feel myself about to weaken. I had to walk home from the station as I had nothing in my pocket. As I walked I heard someone running behind me and calling my name. I didn't recognise him at first, but it was an old school friend of years ago. We talked as he walked home with me. At the gate he stopped and found his wallet. He pulled out fifty pounds and gave it to me. When we were in our last year at school the two of us had a small. business going together selling biscuits and fruit to the kids at school. When we left he had reckoned up and found we had made a profit of fifty pounds over the year. He told me he would bring my share when he came back from holiday, but before he could do that his father was suddenly promoted and the family left with him. I had completely forgotten all about it. It was great, I could pay back my dad the twenty pounds I had borrowed from him and five pounds for the rest of the week, it meant I had twenty five pounds left. I felt very rich as I came here on the bus. Then I had an idea. You had told us about tything, so 10% of that money was five pounds. What should I do with it? How should I tythe it? Then I had a brilliant idea. I will give it to the person I sit next to in class."

Everyone applauded him, but when the girl explained what we had been doing and her own situation, there was almost pandemonium. Cheering, laughing, hugging and endless talk was the order of the night. I said, "Let's have a celebration." So we all went to the canteen and coffee and cake was on me!

A 3-step pattern.

1. Each day write out the thing you want most in your life at this moment. A small goal.

2. Mentally image the thing that you want. Make the picture as real as you can Use a visual aid.

3. Boldly and deliberately command the successful result to appear.

If you work every day on these three simple steps the good that you seek will overflow into your life!

KEY 5. WATCH YOUR WORDS!

SECTION 3. THINKING = BEING.

Affirmations are words of power. The word affirm means to make firm. We make firm a goal we so greatly desire by saying an affirmation describing our goal, thus firming it in our mind.

Affirmations are important. When we say an affirmation we are conditioning our mind: in exactly the same way we were originally conditioned in early childhood by the people around us. By affirming the things you want in your life you are simply doing what was done to you years ago, only this time you choose what is said.

The Jesuits said—give me the child until he is seven and I have the man.

You are no longer a three or four year old child. You now have the choice as to what you accept in your mind and what you discard.

Do not feel guilty about this, you had no choice in the matter as a child, but you do now

GIGO = GARBAGE IN, GARBAGE OUT in computer talk.

So the garbage that was programmed into your mind as a child will only produce garbage results unless you change it.

GIGO = GOOD IN, GOOD OUT!

You are in control and you can programme yourself to be exactly the kind of person you want to be. If you are shy and retiring you can become an outgoing, friendly person, full of energy and enthusiasm. Through affirmations we are working with the basic law of the mind, "As a man thinketh in his heart, so is he."

We are merely substituting the word 'subconscious' for 'heart'. It is not the thinking that is done on the surface of the mind that strongly affects us, it is the heart thinking, or to put it another way, it is the conditioning of the patterns of thought, action, beliefs and attitudes. Most important of all, remember that the thinking comes first then the being.

You will be what you think.

A very simple way to remember this mind formula which operates as exactly as any mathematical formula is:

THINKING = BEING

At this stage it does not matter if you believe the affirmations or not, it is only necessary to DO them. At first you will have a great disbelief, but each day the disbelief will get smaller and smaller until at one point you will get a very small belief. Then, as you keep on saying the affirmations your belief will get bigger and bigger until, a short time later, you will actually BELIEVE your affirmations and you are then programmed positively!

One young student, an ex heroin addict, was told by various doctors that she would never be able to have a child. It was her dearest wish to have a child, but as the months passed the tests were negative. Early one morning her husband woke up and found she was not in bed. He rushed downstairs and found her in the kitchen just about to inject herself with heroin. Her mother brought her to see me and we talked. She agreed to come each week and take things one step at a time.

A few months passed and still she could not conceive. But, she was no longer depressed. I had told her of a past student who had been told that she and her husband were both infertile and would never have children. It took fifteen months for this couple to conceive and they now have two very healthy children. The young student was so taken with this story she worked very conscientiously with everything I gave her. She said, "I believe you." I told her not to believe me but to believe in the principles with which she was working. Her reply was, "I believe you because you care about me and you have proved these things yourself. I cannot trust myself yet, so I know I have a lot of work to do. I do trust you though."

She grinned at me as though she was throwing down a challenge. I decided to ignore that and we carried on working.

Last week she gave birth to a lovely, healthy boy. During her pregnancy she visualised her baby as being perfectly formed and healthy. She surrounded herself and her baby with white light and knew, without any doubts, that the baby would be perfect.

And he is! The medical staff are amazed that she could conceive let alone have such a wonderful baby.

She needed to believe. She could not believe in herself because everyone around her felt she was no good and would never make it. Heroin deadened the pain.

She trusted me and she believed me.

So if you have any difficulty, TRUST! The wonderful, creative power of your SCM will work for you once you know what to do.

A lot of people know about these principles but they do not demonstrate success and happiness in their lives. Why? Because they do not *use* the laws. They have the knowledge and leave it there. They do not *use* the knowledge, put it into practice in their own lives. So they miss out on life.

When making affirmations certain rules must be followed.

1. **They must be stated positively.** You must have positive goals for your life and you must have positive affirmations to match them.

 e.g. If your goal is for more courage your affirmation should be : "I am courageous in all situations." It is not correct to say, "I am not afraid anymore." This is a negative statement.

2. **They must be said and written in the present tense.** Your SCM will literally accept all words at their face value, so it is important to use present tense only.

It is negative and incorrect to say, "I am going to be a confident person." Using this kind of statement denotes the future not the present and you will never achieve your goals, you will always be going to achieve them in the future. You know the old saying, "tomorrow never comes," well your goals will never come that way.

"I am a confident person." This is the correct way to affirm. You are confident NOW. The present tense.

3. **They must be fully written down.** This is necessary for two reasons. FIRST. When you write out your affirmations you are making a brain cell impression.

SECOND. Affirmations are apt to be forgotten unless they are written down.

4. **All your goals must be written down as affirmations.** Do not make the mistake of lumping all your goals together in an affirmation, such as, "I am a rich, healthy, happy person." This will simply not work. Make a separate, clear, concise, complete affirmation for each goal.

There are two ways of affirming. You affirm verbally and you affirm visually. You speak and you visualise or picture what you want. Your words used with your mental pictures make very powerful affirmations.

What you believe about yourself becomes your reality. Your life right now is the result of your past beliefs. You can change it.

When we first start working with these principles we feel we are believing, in fact we say, "I believe". This belief is only a shallow belief, it exists only in our CM. This aspect of our mind is the intellect which has grasped the idea and knows it has. Unless the idea is worked with consistently and practically it will always remain in the mind as an idea and it will finally be erased. An idea must go beneath the conscious mind down to the depths of our SCM into the fertile powerhouse which is always ready to receive our instructions. Once you believe in your heart (SCM) then things begin to happen.

You cannot obviously think with your heart. You do that with your intellect. If you think constantly over a period of time, that thinking becomes firm in your SCM and it is acted upon.

We can sometimes mistake an emotion for a firm conviction. For instance, a few of our students become very excited and overcome by the truth of what they hear in the first session. Their eyes shine and they are full of enthusiasm and say with total conviction, "I believe it." Their hearts are stirred by it all but they are not necessarily stirred into creative, forceful action.

The heart, the SCM, can only be stirred or reached by our words. Every word we utter and every silent word (thought) held in our mind is a directive to our SCM and it is acted upon.

So if we say "I believe" many many times we are giving an order which becomes stronger each time we say it.

The early students start well but do not persist. Their progress suffers until they understand.

If you say "I believe" then perhaps a couple of hours later, or maybe a day later you countermand that statement by saying, "I am afraid" or "I don't feel well" or "I can't do it" and other things like this, then you do not really believe.

It is the law of consistency which is the key to success.

All your statements, either your words which you speak out loud or, the words in thought, must be of the same pattern, they must be positive and constructive.

A superficial belief is rather like trying to switch on the light with will-power instead of using your hand on the switch.

Try to visualise this:

Every positive word and thought turns on a light in your heart.

Every negative word and thought turns it out!

KEY 5. WATCH YOUR WORDS.

SECTION 4. POW!

Spoken words are powerful, whether they are positive or negative. The sound of the spoken word vibrates and causes things to happen. We must be selective in the choice of words we use. Idle, thoughtless words, joking words, insincere words, angry cutting words, are just as potent as kind, loving, positive, constructive words. Thoughtless words cause our problems. Negative thoughts and words cause negative vibrations and these negative vibrations bring about negative happenings in our lives.

Have you ever been introduced to a stranger to whom you felt an instant dislike? Or, have you entered a room filled with. people and felt uncomfortable? Your SCM is picking up the vibrations of other people and a lot of these vibes are incompatible with your wavelength. I think it was Emerson who said, "WHAT YOU ARE SPEAKS SO LOUDLY I CANNOT HEAR WHAT YOU SAY."

We are all constantly transmitting and receiving vibrations caused by our own thoughts and words. The vibratory power of words releases within yourself whatever you decree, command or say. The word "utter" and the word "outer" have the same root meaning, so what you "utter" becomes the "outer" part of your life, your reality.

Good, positive, constructive words spoken with a firm command and belief will clear away old, negative thought patterns that have crowded your mind and your emotions. There are layers upon layers of thought patterns in your mind, rather like the layers of skin on an onion, which need clearing out, which must be peeled away before you can achieve your goals. Creative constructive words spoken with feeling and belief will clear away the old garbage. It only takes patience and persistence and a determination to succeed.

Whenever my children went to the seaside they would always collect shells and pebbles to take home. Over the years we had quite a collection of these and I got a little tired of dusting them. One rainy day my elder daughter decided to paint some pebbles. She held each one in her hand for a time and then let her intuition decide what should be painted. The results were extraordinary. Some shapes suggested flowers, others animals, some were futuristic. She then decided to paint one for her young brother. After careful thought she chose a large, smooth, oval-shaped pebble and simply wrote the word POW! on it. This word was done in bright colours and it stood out from all the rest. I asked her why she had written it.

"It is short for POWER and he will feel good when he sees it."

True enough, my son loved it and still has it to this day.

Whenever I saw that pebble lying there it gave me quite a boost, it reminded me that I have the power within myself to do anything I think I can. I have since given children the opportunity to paint their own pebbles and parents are amazed at the results and particularly the messages the kids write on their pebbles.

WORDS ARE POWERFUL SO CHOOSE THEM WISELY!

The three most powerful words in the world are, I LOVE YOU!

The words. I HATE YOU, are just as powerful in the wrong way.

Whenever you feel inadequate or unable to cope with a situation try this affirmation:

**"I can handle it,
I am powerful,
I am full of power.
My inner power now works wonders in my life."**

This is an affirmation of command and it must be said out loud with great command and feeling. Repeat it over and over until you are really saying it with vehemence, then let it go.

IMPORTANT!

Do not think about it again. Make yourself busy, do anything to take your mind off it. Like posting a letter, you put it in the post box and forget it. You do not keep wondering if it will get there, YOU TRUST! If you start thinking of the desired result and wondering how, when and where it will come, you are not trusting You will destroy what you desire most in your life.

Lack of trust means doubt and you are doubting the power of your own inner self, your wonderful SPCM.

Repeat this affirmation every night and every morning with firmness, strong persistence and patience.

Keep on doing it regardless of any evidence or lack of evidence until you know without a shadow of doubt that it is so.

We all have to learn to trust and believe in ourselves. This is a personal thing, it is not something you can delegate to others. You must learn to trust your own inner power, your intuition. It takes time and patience to eradicate all the wrong and unhealthy thought patterns in your SCM so slowly does it. This is not something that you can do overnight. It is rather like water dripping on a stone, it will eventually wear away the stone. Your mind was programmed in the same way, by the constant dripping of negative words and actions from the time you were born. These cannot be erased in a flash. There must be a daily working on yourself with affirmations and visualisations and complete trust.

Begin to talk to your SCM ask it questions. You have access to all the wisdom of the universe through the power of your SCM so do not be afraid to ask it for guidance. Ask, "What is the truth about this situation? Make it so clear that I cannot mistake it." This is what people mean when they ask for a sign.

The sign will come, usually in unexpected ways. But once you have asked, then you must release it, let it go and trust. There must be no wondering about it, use your energy to keep on affirming that it will come.

Once when we moved to a new area I tried to get a local

teaching post. Interviews were good and in each instance they wanted to appoint me. Unfortunately there was pressure to take an existing member of staff so I did not get any of the posts I had applied for.

I decided to ask for guidance from my SCM I did this very firmly then I let it go. I then forgot about it as I worked hard in the garden as it was the summer holiday.

A week later I opened the paper at situations vacant and an advert seemed to leap out from the page toward me. It was for a Head of the English department at a Secondary school a few miles away in the country.

I applied and two days later the Head rang me and we talked. I went to see him the following morning and during the afternoon I was interviewed together with six other applicants. I got the job! When I actually started work I found the reason why I was appointed. The department was so run down and the teaching was pathetic. There had been no specialist teacher for two years. I completely reorganised everything, introduced drama into the curriculum, entered pupils for all exams and for the County Festival of Speech and Creative Writing. The results astounded even me! The students all learned to relax and let the creative power within themselves work and the results were astonishing. One girl who left school wrote a book. No one had realised she had the latent talent which was lying dormant.

We can never know what possibilities there are ahead of us, unless we learn to use this amazing power within us. We must learn to trust it. It keeps us alive and our body functioning perfectly without any assistance from us.

You have your own special talents and abilities which no one else shares. You are unique. You should never feel that you must go along with the crowd or do what some other person thinks you should do. You will be going against your own nature, you will be relinquishing your own power to others, you will be opting out of your responsibility for your own life.

You need the sense of achievement which accompanies the completion of a task or goal. It is the way you are made. You are born to be successful in all aspects of your life.

These exercises must be done in a light hearted manner, there must be no strain or anxiety because this will destroy your efforts.

I CAN IF I THINK I CAN!

I AM MASTER OF MY OWN LIFE.

I GIVE THANKS FOR THE GREAT POWER WITHIN MY SCM. IT IS JUST WAITING FOR ME TO USE IT WISELY!

QUESTIONS.

1. Why is it important to command our good?

2. Why is it important to trust?

3. What is the reason for matching words to mental pictures?

4. What is the price you have to pay for success?

5. Why do we need to say affirmations?

6. What is the mind formula?

7. What are the two ways of affirming?

8. How should the affirmation of command be said?

9. How can you really find out what you deeply desire?

10. How can a sign come?

SUNSPOTS

**KEEP YOUR MIND ON
THE THINGS YOU WANT
AND OFF THE THINGS
YOU DON'T WANT!**

KEY 6. I AM AFRAID...

SECTION 1. WHAT DO I FEAR?

Before you can be successful at anything your mind must be ready to receive it. Your mind can only receive when it has been prepared to receive. There are three enemies which you must clear out of your mind—indecision, doubt and fear. Your intuitive sense will not be able to function until you clear these three negatives out.

These three are members of an unholy trio and are related to each other. Where one is found the other two are always close by.

Indecision is the seedling of fear. Remember this.

Indecision crystalises into **doubt;** these two blend and become **fear.**

The blending process is slow and this is a reason why these three enemies are so dangerous. They **germinate** and **grow** without their presence being observed.

You are unaware of what is happening inside you.

The purpose of this lesson is to turn the spotlight of attention upon the cause and cure of the enemy. Before we can master an enemy, we must know its name, its habits, and where it resides. There are six basic fears and we will deal with each one of them as thoroughly as we can and maybe you will be able to see which of them if not all of them, refer to you. Sometimes these enemies remain hidden in our SCM where they are difficult to locate and eliminate. So time spent on this is time well spent.

There are six basic fears which most of us suffer from at some time or other, or with many combinations of these.

POVERTY, CRITICISM, ILL-HEALTH, LOST LOVE, OLD AGE, DEATH.

They are named in order of their most common appearance. The first three are at the bottom of most of our worries.

Fears are nothing more than states of mind.
We can control our state of mind. Man can create nothing which he does not first conceive in the form of an impulse of thought. These thought impulses begin immediately to translate themselves into their physical equivalent.
A state of mind is something that must be created, you cannot buy it.

POVERTY.

Fear of poverty is a state of mind, nothing else. But it is enough to destroy your chance of achieving success. This fear paralyses your faculties of reason and imagination; it undermines your enthusiasm; kills off self-reliance; discourages initiative; leads to uncertainty of purpose; encourages procrastination; and makes self-control impossible. It clouds the memory and invites failure in every conceivable form. I could go on and on like this.

The fear of poverty is the most destructive of all the basic fears. It is also the most difficult to master. The fear of poverty grew out of man's tendency to prey upon his fellow man economically. Animals are motivated by instinct, their capacity to think is limited so they prey upon each other, physically. Man, with his superior intellect and intuition, does not eat his fellow man bodily, he gets his satisfaction out of eating him financially. Man is so avaricious that every conceivable law has been passed to safeguard him from his fellow man. Nothing brings man so much suffering and humility as poverty. So it is no wonder he fears it! Man has learned from past experiences that some people cannot be trusted where matters of money and earthly possessions are concerned.

So eager is man to possess wealth that he will get it through whatever means he can, legal or otherwise.

If we demand more from life than mediocrity and poverty we must do some self-analysis to show the weaknesses we do not want to recognise within ourselves. We are after the truth. Only a courageous analysis will show the presence of this universal enemy. Search deeply into your character.

Symptoms that show fear of poverty.

1. *INDIFFERENCE.* Usually expressed through lack of ambition; a willingness to tolerate poverty; accepting without protest everything life offers; mental and physical laziness; a lack of imagination, initiative, enthusiasm and self-control.

2. *INDECISION.* The habit of allowing other people to do your thinking for you. A 'sitting on the fence'.

3. *DOUBT.* Always making excuses or alibis to cover up, explain away, or apologise for one's failures. Sometimes expressed in the form of envy for those who are successful, by criticising them.

4. *WORRY.* There is a tendency to find fault with others; to spend beyond one's income; there could be a neglect of personal appearance; scowling and frowning; nervousness and lack of confidence and poise; and there maybe a tendency to drink, drugs, over eating and excessive smoking.

5. *OVERCAUTIOUS.* The habit of looking for the negative in everything. Thinking and talking of possible failure, instead of looking for the possibilities in each situation. Knowing all the roads to disaster, but never once searching for the plan to avoid failure. Waiting for the right time to begin putting the ideas and plans into action. Only remembering the people who have failed, not those who have succeeded. Seeing the hole in the doughnut, but overlooking the doughnut. Pessimism which leads to indigestion, constipation, bad breath and a bad disposition.

6. *PROCRASTINATION.* The habit of putting off until tomorrow what should have been done last year. Refusal to accept responsibility when it can be avoided. Willingness to compromise rather than put up a stiff fight for what you want; compromising with difficulties instead of using them as stepping stones to advancement. Planning what to do if and when you are overtaken by failure, instead of 'burning your boats' and making retreat impossible. A total lack of self confidence, self control, ambition, enthusiasm, initiative, thrift and sound reasoning ability. Expecting poverty

instead of demanding riches. Associating with others who accept poverty, instead of seeking the company of people who demand and receive riches.

The vibrations of fear pass from one mind to another just as quickly as the sound of the human voice passes from the BBC station to the receiver your radio. Negative thoughts and words produce a negative 'kick-back' which breaks down the faculty of creative imagination. It also produces a negative personality, which repels people. And don't forget, these negs will lodge very firmly in the SCM. These then become part of your character.

You are here to be successful, healthy, wealthy, happy and fulfilled. So you must find peace of mind and freedom from the fears that are embedded in your SCM. Success begins with thoughts and words of success.

Susceptibility to negative influences.

Throughout our lives we are surrounded by negative influences which are so subtle we are not aware they are there.

Sometimes the well meant words of a relative or friend are negative but we do not recognise them as such unless we are constantly on our guard against them. Our own mental attitude, which is made up of all suggestions and advice from the day we were born, actually makes us susceptible, as the SCM never sleeps and is forever feeding into our CM all the negs we are programmed with.

Your Will Power.

To protect yourself from negative influences, whether they are of your own making or from others around you, recognise that you have a will power and put it into constant use until it builds a wall of immunity against influences in your own mind.

All human beings are by nature, lazy, indifferent and highly susceptible to all suggestions which harmonise with their weaknesses.

We are all susceptible to the six basic fears so we must learn to counteract them.

Keep your mind closed to all people who depress or discourage you in any way. Clean out your medicine chest and throwaway all pills and medicines and stop pandering to colds, headaches, pains and imaginary illness. Deliberately seek the company of people who influence you to think and act for yourself. Do not expect troubles as they have a tendency not to disappoint!

What is your greatest worry! Why do you tolerate it?

KEY 6. I AM AFRAID...

SECTION 2. THE GREATEST ENEMY.

Fear is man's greatest enemy. Fear is behind failure, sickness, and poor human relations. Millions of people are afraid of the past, the future and the unknown. Fear is a thought in your mind, so you are afraid of your own thoughts! As a child I was paralysed by fear because my brother told me there was a bogeyman who would spring out and get me.

For weeks I was so afraid I clung to my mother wherever she went, just in case this bogeyman sprang out from somewhere and got me. My brother had not described what it looked like or where it was, but what he said and the way he said it was quite enough for my childish imagination to work overtime in the wrong way. My mother finally grew tired of me always scuttling behind her she demanded to know what was wrong. I was too scared to have any loyalty to my brother and so relieved to be able to tell her, I blurted out the whole thing.

After she had finished with my brother and then me—I was left in no doubt at all that I had accepted without question all that had been told to me and that I had to start questioning everything I was not sure about in future and above all, I had to ask her, my mother, as she knew a lot more than any child.

The thing I feared did not exist. Fear is simply a shadow of the mind and shadows have no reality.

Do the thing you fear to do and the death of fear is certain.

Ralph Waldo Emerson

When I first started Public Speaking I was filled with total fear as I stood in front of an audience. The only way I could overcome this fear was to keep on doing it. I also affirmed that I was the master, not fear, and kept visualising myself speaking publicly with ease and confidence. Fear was simply a shadow of my mind which I refused to recognise.

How to conquer fear.

For five minutes, three or four times a day:

Sit in a comfortable chair and relax your body. Mentally see yourself actually doing the thing you fear to do. Make the mental picture as real as you can, fill in all the details. Then, see someone you like and respect coming to you to congratulate you on your success. Again make this congratulation as real as you can. By doing this you are experiencing in your imagination what will go into your SCM and eventually will become a reality in your life.

Before you open your eyes after visualisation, always say, "It is done," and then give thanks. When we do this in class the response is tremendous and students do this very often during the day and they get fantastic results.

One young student does not take a coffee break. He goes to the loo and locks himself in for at least five minutes. He sits there and does his visualisation. He says it works wonders, he can now cope with rude customers and bad-tempered staff without being upset in any way. He also added, amidst hoots of laughter from the class, that not once has anyone tried to get in the loo when he is visualising. He said it is as if people know not to disturb him although he has never told anyone about what he is doing. He has pinpointed and conquered three fears this way.

Man is born with two fears; the fear of falling and the fear of loud noises. This is natures alarm system as a means of self-preservation. This is normal fear. You hear a car coming down the road but you may not see it. You stop until it goes by before stepping off the kerb. You do that for your survival. Your momentary fear of being run over is overcome by your action. All your other fears were given to you by parents, teachers, friends etc who influenced your early years. Abnormal fear is when man allows his imagination to run riot. There are many people who are afraid that something dreadful will happen to their children, They vividly picture this happening. This is abnormal fear. There are others who read about, or see on TV, a terrible epidemic or rare disease and they live in total fear that they will catch it. Some actually imagine they already have the disease. This is abnormal fear.

If you stay with this abnormal fear, you will stagnate and then mentally and physically deteriorate.

When fear arises there immediately comes also a desire for something opposite to the fear. Immediately place your attention on this opposite thing desired and do not dwell on the fear.

Put simply, dwell on the good, not the bad. Whatever you dwell on will become stronger and stronger. If you give strength to fear by constantly dwelling on it you are lost.

Get absorbed and engrossed in the desire, knowing that the subjective always overcomes the objective. This attitude will give you confidence and lift your spirits. The great power of your SCM is moving on your behalf, and it cannot fail. So peace and assurance are yours.

DO YOU FEAR CRITICISM?

Man has this fear in a highly developed form. It maybe part of man's inherited nature(the race mind)which prompts him not only to take away his fellow man's goods, but to justify his actions by criticising the other man's character. It is a well known fact that a thief will criticise the man from whom he steals. That politicians seek office not by displaying their own talents and qualifications, but by attempting to belittle their opponents and criticising them personally.

Criticism is the one form of service of which everyone has too much. Our nearest relatives are usually the ones who criticise us the most. Parents are the worst offenders. Constant and unnecessary criticism of a child will build an inferiority complex that will inhibit the child for life, and maybe worse. Criticism plants resentment and fear into the human heart, it does not build love or affection.

To get the best out of people and that includes children, constructive suggestion rather than criticism will pay great dividends.

IF A CHILD IS CRITICISED HE LEARNS TO CONDEMN.

This fear is almost as universal as the fear of poverty. Its effects are just as fatal to personal achievement because it destroys initiative and discourages the use of imagination.

7 symptoms that show fear of criticism.

1. SELF-CONSCIOUSNESS. Generally expressed through timidity, nervousness, timidity in conversation and with strangers. Awkward movements of the hands and limbs and shifting of the eyes.

2. LACK OF POISE. Expressed through lack of voice control, nervousness in the presence of others. Poor body posture and poor memory.

3. WEAK PERSONALITY. Lacks firmness of decision, has no personal charm, Agrees with others without careful examination of their opinions. Sidesteps issues instead of meeting them head on.

4. INFERIORITY COMPLEX. Using 'big words' to impress others without knowing the meaning. Boasting of imaginary achievements. Imitates the speech, dress and manners of others. Boasting.

5. EXTRAVAGANCE. Spending beyond one's income. Unwise use of credit cards. Trying to keep up with the Joneses.

6. LACK OF INITIATIVE. Failure to see opportunities for advancement.

Fear to express opinions. Lack of confidence in one's own ideas. Giving evasive answers to questions asked by superiors. Hesitancy of manner and speech. Deceitful in words and deeds.

7. LACK OF AMBITION. Mental and physical laziness. Lack of self assertion. Too easily influenced. Criticising others behind their backs and flattering them to their faces. Accepting defeat without protest. Suspicion of other people without cause. Lack of tact in manner and speech. Unwillingness to accept the blame for mistakes.

Fear of criticism can also be tied to our need for love and acceptance.

Work on the ones that touch you inside as you read them.

Have courage to bring out the fears and face them. Then give your sole attention to the opposite of the fear.

If the fear thought returns, immediately think the opposite. In time, if you do this persistently, you will feel at peace and much more confident and alive.

KEY 6. I AM AFRAID...

SECTION 3. ILL HEALTH & LOST LOVE.

Basically, the fear of ill-health is related to the fear of death. Man fears ill-health because of the terrible pictures which have been planted in his mind of what may happen if death should overtake him. He also fears it because of the economic burden of long illness etc on the family.

Over 75% of all people who visit doctors are suffering from Hypochondria(imaginary illness) It has been proved that the fear of disease, even when there is not the slightest cause for fear, will produce the physical symptoms of the disease feared.

The human mind is powerful and mighty. It builds or it destroys!

The fear of ill-health, this common weakness of mankind, has helped the chemists and drug companies to make tremendous fortunes.

People can be made ill by suggestion. Disease begins in the form of a negative thought impulse. Such an impulse can be passed from one mind to another by suggestion, or created by an individual in his own mind. The seed of fear of ill-health lives in everyone.

Worry, discouragement, fear, disappointment, cause this seed to germinate and grow. Disappointment heads the list of causes of fear of ill-health.

A change of mental attitude is the cure for all fears.

I never suffer from colds, flu, or any other form of 'winter illness simply because I do not accept it. If an epidemic is raging, it does not touch me or my family. We do not want it in our lives so we do not accept it.

We did an experiment in class. Three people agreed to be the questioners. No one in the class knew what it was all about and it covered a period of a few weeks. The three people were to ask a question, "What is the matter? you look very ill." The first person asked the question, then after a short time period the second one asked the same question to the same person. The third person asked the question after another suitable tide lapse.

Each class member was asked this question by the three people at different times so that they did not connect the questioners. they did not only ask during or after the meeting, but on the way home, or as the student arrived, or even at a casual meeting.

Notes were taken and it was done in a very logical manner. Each class member was asked the same question by three different people and at different times and circumstances. I felt it was a masterpiece of planning on their part.

The findings were astonishing. All the class members with one exception, reacted the same way. At the first question they looked in disbelief and said, "I'm alright, there is nothing wrong." The second question, by a different person, brought the answer,

"I don't know, I feel awful."

The third result was answered, "I feel very ill."

After class discussion, students realised how easily one is influenced by suggestion. Most of them said they did feel ill after the second and third question. They felt that if three people could see illness then they must be ill!

They began to analyse advertising to see how much that influenced their buying of various products. After all that, they emerged a great deal stronger in character and more able to deal with the suggestions of others.

7 SYMPTOMS THAT SHOW FEAR OR ILL-HEALTH.

1. AUTOSUGGESTION. Looking for and expecting to find symptoms of all kinds of disease. Enjoying imaginary illness and speaking about it as though it were real. Trying all kinds of 'cures'. Constantly talking about operations, accidents, illnesses. Experimenting with diets, physical exercise and all kinds of reducing systems, without professional advice.

2. HYPOCHONDRIA. Talking about and concentrating the mind on diseases. Expecting the appearance of

disease. Most cases of 'nerves' come from imaginary illness. The only cure for this negative thinking is the opposite, positive thinking

3. INDOLENCE. Fear of ill-health often brings about laziness which interferes with proper physical exercise. The result, overweight.

4. SUSCEPTIBILITY. This fear causes a breakdown of the body's immune system which lowers one's resistance to disease.

5. SELF-CODDLING. There is a bid for sympathy here, using imaginary illness. People often use this to avoid work. The habit of pretending illness to cover plain laziness or as an alibi for lack of ambition.

6. INTEMPERANCE. The habit of using alcohol or drugs to kill pain such as headaches, neuralgia etc., instead of eliminating the cause.

7. WORRY. The habit of reading about illness and worrying about the possibility of getting it. Reading all the advertisements for medicines and cures.

DO YOU FEAR THE LOSS OF LOVE?

The original source of this fear grew out of man's habit of stealing his fellow-man's mate. Jealousy and other painful neuroses grew out of man's inherited fear of the loss of love. This fear is the most painful of all the six basic fears and it plays more havoc with the body and mind than any of the other fears.

This fear probably dates back to the Stone Age when men stole women by brute force. Man's habits are the same now as they were at the dawn of civilisation, but he expresses them differently. Instead of force he now uses persuasion— the promise of jewels, clothes, furs, business opportunities etc. These are much more effective than brute force.

Women are more susceptible to this fear than men. Women have learned from experience that men are by nature polygamous, that they are not to be trusted in the hands of rivals.

This is not putting men down. Nature has given man a very powerful sex-drive as a means of procreation of the species. Women therefore have to work harder than men to keep a good relationship going.

The distinguishing features of this fear are:

1. JEALOUSY. The habit of being suspicious of friends and loved ones without sufficient grounds. The habit of accusing a mate of infidelity without sufficient grounds. General suspicion of everyone. Cannot trust anyone.

2. FAULT FINDING. The habit of finding fault with loved ones, friends, relatives, business associates at the slightest provocation, or without any cause whatsoever.

3. GAMBLING. The habit of gambling, stealing, cheating and taking hazardous chances to provide money for loved ones, with the belief that love can be bought. Spending beyond ones means and incurring debts to provide gifts for loved ones, to make a favourable showing. Insomnia, nervousness, lack of persistence, weakness of will, lack of self-control, lack of self-reliance, bad temper, are all symptoms of feeling unloved.

I had a private student, a very rich man, whose problem was gambling. He had gambled his fortune away. The reason? He feared his wife would leave him.

He and his wife were of different nationalities, so there were many difficulties in that direction. Both were rigid towards each other. Each wanted the other to change, without any attempt to change their own attitudes. For a time things got better, but now the wife has left him and he is totally destroyed. Even now there is no attempt to compromise. Both are rigid. Only time will tell the outcome.

The thing I feared has come upon me, said Job.

KEY 6. I AM AFRAID...

SECTION 4. OLD AGE AND DEATH.

The fear of old age grows out of two sources. First is the thought that old age may bring poverty and ill-health. The second and this is by far the most common source, from false and cruel teachings of the past which have been too well mixed with 'hell fire' and other bogies which were cunningly designed to keep man obedient through fear.

In the basic fear of old age man has two very sound reasons for his apprehension. One growing out of his distrust of his fellow man, who may seize whatever worldly goods he may possess; and the other arising from the terrible pictures in his mind of the next world. Eroticism also enters into this fear of old age. No one cherishes the thought of diminishing sex drive or sexual attraction.

The most common cause of this fear is associated with the possibility of poverty. It throws a chill into the mind of every person having to face declining years in poverty.

Another contributing cause for this fear is the possibility of loss of freedom and independence. Old age may bring with it the loss of both physical and economic freedom.

THE COMMONEST SYMPTOMS OF THIS FEAR ARE:

1. PREMATURE SLOWDOWN. The tendency to slow down around the age of 40—the age of mental maturity—and to develop an inferiority complex. Falsely believing one's self to be slipping because of age.

2. APOLOGY FOR ONE'S AGE. The habit of speaking apologetically of one's self as being old merely because one has reached the age of 40 or 50. Instead one should feel and express gratitude for having reached the age of wisdom and understanding.

3. KILLING OFF INITIATIVE. Initiative, imagination and self-reliance are lost when one falsely believes he or she is too old to exercise these qualities.

4. 'MUTTON DRESSED AS LAMB' Trying to appear

younger by dressing as teenagers and copying younger people in their mannerisms, style and speech. People only ridicule this kind of behaviour. One must be true to oneself. This does not mean conforming to what other people expect from you. Modern styles look good on any age group.

There are so many compensations for growing older. We have no need to try in a frantic effort to clutch tightly onto our youth.

Consider film stars and people who have large sums of money to waste on plastic surgery. They can have bits chopped off here and there, in fact faces are not only lifted but altered completely. Bodies are also cut down to size. What for? So that person can be admired and acclaimed?

Whatever is altered on the outside does not change the person. Inside, these people still have the fears and neuroses that decided them to change their appearance. They are still unhappy people. They are unable to come to terms with themselves. There is no real happiness or peace within.

DO YOU FEAR DEATH?

For thousands of years man has been asking "Where did I come from and where am I going?"

In the darker ages of the past the cunning and crafty were not slow to answer these questions, to their own advantage. The possibility of descending into hell caught hold of the imagination in such a realistic way, it paralysed reason and set up a fear of death.

The fear of death is not as common now as it used to be. Better education for all has dispelled the fears of the dark ages.

The world is made up of only two things, energy and matter. In elementary physics we learn that neither matter nor energy (the only two realities known to man) can be created or destroyed. Both matter and energy can be transformed, but neither can be destroyed.

Life is energy. If neither energy nor matter can be destroyed, then life cannot be destroyed. Life, like other forms of energy, may be passed through various processes of transition or change, but it cannot be destroyed.

Death is mere transition.

If death is not mere change or transition, then nothing comes after death except a long, eternal, peaceful sleep, and sleep is nothing to be feared. So you can wipe out forever this fear of death.

SYMPTOMS THAT SHOW FEAR OF DEATH.

1. THINKING ABOUT DYING. This habit is more prevalent among the aged, but young people often think of dying instead of making the most of life. Often this is due to a lack of purpose. The greatest remedy for fear of death is a burning desire for achievement, backed by useful service to others. A busy person does not think of dying.

2. ASSOCIATION WITH FEAR OF POVERTY. We can fear the onset of poverty in our own life or we can fear that our death will bring poverty to our loved ones.

3. ASSOCIATION WITH ILLNESS OR IM-BALANCE. Physical illness may lead to mental depression. Disappointment in love; religious fanaticism; a high state of neurosis or actual insanity, are other causes of the death fear. The six basic fears become translated into a state of worry through indecision. You can relieve yourself forever of the fear of death by reaching a decision to accept death as a change of the physical state. a transition.

Know, with absolute certainty, that the life force within you does not die, it cannot be destroyed, only changed.

YOUR SCM DOES NOT GROW OLD.

Your SCM is timeless, ageless and endless. It is part of the universal Consciousness which was never born and will never die.

Medical science has proved that years alone are not responsible for bringing about aging and the degenerative disorders. It is the fear of time that has a harmful aging effect on our minds and bodies, not time itself. The neurotic fear of the effects of time is the cause of premature aging and early death.

Many people are afraid of what they call, old age, which means to them the end and extinction. This really means that they are afraid of life. Yet, life is endless. **Age is not the flight of years, but the dawn of wisdom.**

Wisdom is an awareness of the tremendous spiritual power in your SCM and the knowledge of how to apply these powers to lead a full and happy life. Get it out of your head once and for all that, 60, 70, 80 or 90 years of age is synonymous with the end for you or anyone else. It can be the beginning of a glorious, active, fruitful and most productive life pattern, better than you have ever experienced.

Believe this, expect it and your SCM will bring it to pass.

Old age is not a tragic happening. It is change which should be welcomed, as each phase of human life is a step forward on the path which has no end. We have powers which transcend our bodily powers, we have senses which transcend our five physical senses.

Anyone who thinks or believes that the earthly cycle of birth, adolescence, youth, maturity and old age, is all there is to life is to be pitied. Such a person has no anchor, no hope, no vision and to him, life has no meaning.

You grow old when you lose interest in life, when you stop dreaming, when you cease to hunger after new truths and new worlds to conquer. When your mind is open to new ideas and new interests, you will be young and vital.

People who live to be over 100 years have things in common.

They eat fewer calories than most people— 1100 to 1900 a day.

They are never overweight, but neither are they undernourished.

They eat less protein and less animal fat and much less cholesterol.

They get plenty of healthy exercise every day.

They have a youthful attitude and expect to live long.

The 3 laws of life.

DESIRE + BELIEVE + EXPECT.

1. You must **intensely desire** your life goal.
2. You must **deeply believe** you will attain your life goal.
3. You must **confidently expect** that you will surely achieve it.

These factors influence the length of our lives! Fear is a learned experience and we learn it in childhood.

As we said previously, a baby has two fears; a fear of loud noises and a fear of falling.

Sometime during childhood these fears become realities in a child's mind.

For instance, crashes of thunder frighten a child and if the mother or any older child is afraid of thunder the child has his fear consolidated and given reality by the behaviour of the frightened adult.

Again, a young child's first ride in a lift or elevator can cause severe anxiety and consolidate the fear of falling, particularly if he is laughed at and perhaps sees the fear of an adult in that situation.

We have to face our fears and recognise them for what they really are. They are just negative states of mind which we have allowed to become firmly fixed in our own SCM.

Fear is the misuse of your great imagination, it is distorted thought patterns that are firmly lodged in your own mind. You put them there. You gave them permission to haunt you. It is like looking in the mirror and making faces at yourself!

A young student who hated lifts would rather walk upstairs than ride in one. One day she went for an important interview and found the room she wanted was on the twelfth floor. As she was only just on time she decided to take the lift so as not to appear out of breath. The lift stuck between the 9th and 10th floors and she was alone. Sheer panic hit her. She pressed the emergency button to no avail. She started screaming after five minutes had elapsed and no sign of rescue. Finally she began to take deep breaths and then said out loud, "God is with me, everything is OK." She kept repeating this over and over. She said it was amazing how she calmed down and re-pressed the bell. This time it was heard and answered and she arrived ten minutes late for her interview. She was very calm as she apologised and gave the reason for being late. The Board were very sympathetic and congratulated her on her wonderful composure.

She got the job!

She was told later that they admired her composure so much after that ordeal and they knew she would be ideal in an emergency.

She said, "I don't know what made me talk to God, I usually keep that for the end of the day."

That certainly started a class discussion and all the students felt that if we 'talked' to God more often during the day we would not get into as many difficulties.

After that incident the class asked me if I would say a prayer with them before each class began. They thought they would get more out of the lesson.

As it happened they did and not only that they felt more wide awake and energetic and receptive.

Refuse to allow your fears room in your life. They will not help you they will only hinder you.

QUESTIONS.

1. What are the three enemies you must clear out of your mind before you can be successful?
2. What is it that will not be able to function if you do not clear out these enemies?
3. What are the six basic fears of mankind?
4. What is fear? Can we control it? How?
5. What does the fear of poverty do to us?
6. How do we counteract our susceptibility to fear?
7. What does Ralph Waldo Emerson say on the subject of fear
8. What can you do when fear arises?
9. What is the danger of criticism?
10. What are the main causes of the fear of ill-health?
11. What is wisdom?
12. What three factors influence the length of our lives?

If you can relate to any of the basic fears in your own life then now is your opportunity to conquer them
Fear not!

SUNSPOTS

I FEEL HEALTHY!
I FEEL HAPPY!
I FEEL TERRIFIC!

KEY 7. RELAX AND LET GO!

SECTION 1. A QUIET MIND.

The only way to solve your problems calmly, intelligently, logically, is to have a quiet mind.

A quiet mind is the only way to maintain mental composure when problem people are arrogant, insulting and hostile. It is the only way to manage a situation when tempers flare and inflammatory emotions threaten. Keep a quiet mind when others rant and rave, yell and shout in their rather stupid efforts to overwhelm by sheer noise; what they cannot solve by sensible thought. Wait, in silence, bide your time and patiently wait for them to exhaust their emotions against the wall of your impenetrable silence.

Your first step to power—the power to manage yourself, so that you can manage others and eventually manage circumstances is a **QUIET MIND.**

When we go to the Mid-west of the U.S.A. we see everywhere warnings of hurricanes. There are clear instructions as to what to do when it happens. Fortunately, we have never seen one, but our friends have.

In a hurricane, destructive winds whirl violently, except in the centre (the "eye") of the hurricane, which is a place of absolute calm in the very centre of the destructive forces all around it.

What has this to do with a quiet mind? Well it has a lot to do with it. There is a very close relationship between your own eyes and your mind. There is constant action and reaction between your physical eyes and your mind. What you see outwardly is transmitted to your mind for action. Your eyes are also highly emotional. They respond to emotion and they stimulate or relax your mind moods, your emotions.

This is beyond physical vision (outer vision). Eye emotion directly affects your mental pictures and your mind moods (inner vision).

It is very important that you learn to control your eye emotions.

How do your eyes respond to your mind moods? Your eyes weep in grief; your eyes smoulder with resentment; your eyes flash with anger; your eyes flame with hostility. And when they do, they not only respond to your emotions, but they stimulate and escalate the emotions to which they respond—and which they openly express!

By relaxing the intensity of your eye emotions, you can calm the mind moods (inner vision) themselves. This is the first step towards a quiet mind.

Eye control of mind moods is by:

1. Becoming consciously aware of the emotion which your eyes are expressing. Realise that tense eye emotion will stimulate and escalate the mind mood itself. It is action and reaction, one stimulates the other. When you become consciously aware of this it will help you to focus on your emotion so that you can relax it with mind control brought about by eye relaxation.

2. Relax your eyes. You can do this by mental command—by deliberately causing your eyes to feel relaxed. "Blank out" all eye tension. Make your eyes feel blank. Imagine your eyes have a "blank look". Unemotional. Unresponsive. Blank. Completely relaxed, almost asleep.

When your eyes are completely relaxed they **cannot** stimulate escalate, or even sustain violent, uncontrolled emotions of anger, resentment, hate, hostility, anxiety, fear, panic or any high tension emotion. It is psychologically impossible to feel two directly opposite emotions at the same time.

So, by completely relaxing your eyes and "blanking out" all eye emotions, you turn off the high-tension, self-damaging, emotions of anger, anxiety, fear, hate, panic and resentment.

This is controlled by the law of consistency.

If your eyes smoulder with resentment, your mind mood will also be resentful. If your eyes flash with anger, your mind mood will also burn with anger.

YOUR EMOTIONS WILL ALWAYS BE THE

SAME (CONSISTENT) THROUGHOUT YOUR ENTIRE NERVOUS SYSTEM.

By the same law of consistency, if you relax your eyes you then relax your mind mood and so do not experience tension. And, because you do not feel tense, you do not express high tension emotions such as resentment etc.

SIMPLE: RELAX YOUR EYES AND YOU TURN OFF THE TENSE EMOTIONS.

We all have a mental faculty of UNDERSTANDING which is located in the front brain. This is a ganglionic nerve centre which is closely connected with the eyes and the feet.

When we understand we say, "I see, I see." Meaning that the light has dawned, or we have perceived something which previously we did not understand. Poor eyesight is related to lack of understanding. Understanding means 'inner vision' so this is our conscious awareness at any given time.

To understand means to 'stand under' and this refers to the feet.

Think how useful our feet are. Feet, for the majority of people are the most neglected and denigrated part of the body. Ill fitting shoes; unwashed feet and socks; add to the way we think about our feet. "My feet are killing me," is said as though it is the fault of the feet themselves! The nerves of the feet are connected by the central nervous system to the ganglionic nerve centre in the front brain, which we call the faculty of understanding. This is a mind faculty and together, with eleven others, make up the twelve mind powers.

We can only understand something when it becomes part of our awareness. Our awareness means we have actually experienced something, we don't just know it intellectually.

If we have the awareness that every part of our body is important, that the body is a space-suit in which we are travelling, we will automatically take care of it and not abuse it in any way.

Start by being kind to your feet! Your feet are wonderful.

Just think of the heavy burden they carry around. They deserve special treatment. They should be washed every day. After washing they should be massaged with either body oil or hand cream. As you massage each foot slowly, making sure you do each toe separately, talk to them! Say that you are sorry for abusing them and complaining about them; as you massage your big toe remember that this toe is the balancer, it keeps your body balanced on your legs. Praise your feet. They deserve it! If you cannot cut your toe nails very well, then go to a chiropodist. Hard skin should be gently filed with an emery board. After a heavy day, soak your feet. A few years ago I invested in a foot spa, which is very invigorating and, if I have been taking a workshop or seminar for a day, rejuvenates my feet after standing for eight hours at a stretch. I am then ready to dance all night!

Do not strain your eyes with too much TV or reading. Eye strain causes tension and eye tension is relayed throughout your entire nervous system. Eye exercises and looking out into the distance also help to strengthen the eyes after too much close work.

Look after your eyes and your feet and your understanding will grow.

KEY 7. RELAX AND LET GO!

SECTION 2. TROUBLE AND STRIFE.

If we can understand what trouble really is, then we can deal with it. Trouble is neither a reward nor a punishment, it is simply a consequence. Being a consequence, trouble can be avoided by avoiding its cause. Until we get to that perfect state when troubles do not occur we have to learn to accept them and **not let them overwhelm us.** It is our own fault if we allow troubles to overwhelm us.

DO NOT EMOTIONALISE TROUBLE.

Most troubles are not as bad as they seem. They couldn't be! Some people emotionalise their troubles by having a temper tantrum. Temper acts as a stimulant, it is like a convulsive fit; it makes you feel stronger for a time. But for a long time afterwards you are weaker. You are weaker physically, mentally, emotionally and spiritually.

Each emotional outburst to any kind of trouble lowers your resistance to the next. Emotionalised trouble is rather like a large rock at the top of the stairs. Once it starts thudding downwards it cannot be stopped. It continues its disastrous descent until it hits emotional bottom, with a personality-shattering crash!

Trouble is bad enough and should not be made worse by emotion.

We intensify trouble by complaining about it. People go about moaning and exaggerating small troubles, turning molehills into mountains. Every scratch on the hand is not a stab in the heart. Let's not emotionalise our trouble. We have only been scratched not stabbed. Our sensitive feelings have been hurt more that our person. Most people think that their unhappiness is caused by what happened to them. This is not correct. Unhappiness, resentment, fear, anxiety and other unpleasant emotional disturbances are caused by how you FEEL about what happens.

WE CAN CONTROL OUR FEELINGS BY CONTROLLING OUR ACTIONS.

How you feel about whatever happens and how you react to those feelings, will be the direct and principal cause of your unhappiness, anxiety etc.

This also applies to our reactions. We react in one of four ways to every thought, sensation, situation or happening which reaches our consciousness.

1. We OVER REACT—this ranges from a mild state to an extreme state of over reaction. We become emotionally overwhelmed and in a lot of cases, have a heart attack.

2. WE REACT INCONSISTENTLY. We react in a manner which is totally opposite to normally expected and prudent response. e.g. we laugh at danger; we deliberately ignore serious warnings; we are contemptuous of necessary help.

3. NON- REACTION. We neither respond nor react. We do nothing.

4. WE REACT WITH THE CALM, THOUGHTFUL, DELIBERATION OF A QUIET MIND.

Of these four ways of reacting to problems, there are only two which are compatible with success. Numbers 3 and 4.

Inconsistent reacting is abnormal and borders on insanity. So let's focus on OVER REACTION which is what most people do in a crisis.

"A man is not hurt by what happens to him so much— as by his opinion of what happens."

Montaigne.

It is not what happens, but how you feel about it, which really matters to you. So remember, you over-react to your feelings themselves, not to whatever caused the feelings. Over-reaction is caused then by over-sensitive feelings.

THE WAY TO PREVENT OVER-REACTING IS TO STOP BEING OVER-SENSITIVE.

The way to stop being over-sensitive begins by accepting the fact that people, things, situations and events are NOT PERFECT.

Nor, are they provided for your personal approval or pleasure.

Nor, is it your responsibility to demand perfection or to personally attempt to make perfect an obviously imperfect world… filled with obviously imperfect people creating obviously imperfect situations.

So, accept the imperfections of others as you obviously hope they will accept your own imperfections.

DO NOT BE OVER SENSITIVE TO IMPERFECTION AND YOU WILL NOT OVER REACT TO ITS FREQUENT APPEARANCE.

Reality is a world full of people who are busy looking out for themselves and, in the process, may unintentionally jostle you about a bit. Nothing personal. It is just that others are preoccupied with their own problems and purposes.

Being preoccupied with their problems, other people are not particularly concerned about your tender feelings. (neither are you about theirs) **That's how it is, accept it!** . Every day you are going to meet people who talk too much, are selfish, ungrateful, egotistical. Do not be surprised or disturbed by this. There can never be a place without them. So, relax do not be OVER SENSITIVE to imperfection do not get uptight about it do not OVER REACT in disapproval… develop the serene attitude of ACCEPTANCE of what cannot be changed and…**KEEP A QUIET MIND.**

People who over react in resentment and anger are neurotic. They are constantly being bruised by reality and react in resentment and anger.

We have to get tough emotionally.

1. IGNORE IT! You must stop resentment and anger before they start. A good friend of mine says that he never wastes a minute thinking about people he doesn't like. He totally ignores them. All his energy is put into his very successful business.

Noting and nobody can disturb me, I won't let them!

If I meet an annoyance I immediately say to myself the above statement or, **none of this disturbs me.**

2. TURN IT OFF! Relax your eyes. Blank it out. **Turn off your emotions.**

Resentment is trouble in the past tense. Whatever caused your resentment HAS ALREADY HAPPENED and therefore CANNOT BE UNDONE. Since the past cannot be changed and the event cannot be altered, you are left with two options:

3. **Change your attitude** toward the cause of your resentment. Remember, it is not what happens but what you feel about what happens, that is crucial.

4. **Forget it!** No situation can be improved by resentment. It can only be made worse. Always assume that every annoyance is not intentional, then completely ignore it. Resentment does not hurt the person you resent, it hurts you! There is a scorpion in South America which, when angered, becomes so furious that it stings itself with its own poison and dies.

That is rather a fitting climax to anger, because anger is indeed self poison.

Some aspects of anger: When a person is wrong and wont admit it, he often gets angry. But anger only highlights the error and a feeling of guilt follows. If there is a prompt and frank admission of error, then people are less critical and usually have a sympathetic understanding. So disaster is avoided.

Anger is used for emphasis in attracting attention. One can think of the angry mob of strikers who rant and rave and use violence to further their cause. Their systems are poisoned by anger and they cannot see that a peaceful way of seeking what they desire is the right way.

Anger is an emotion that can be controlled.

The greatest remedy for anger is delay, or count to ten before you speak; if very angry, count a hundred.

To laugh at provocation is to demolish it, then to forgive is to forget it entirely. Only you can deal with an insult. First, ignore it. If you cannot ignore it then laugh at it. If you cannot laugh at it then it is probably deserved and you should learn from it.

We learn more from our enemies than from our friends. So even if we cannot love our enemies we shouldn't hate them for they are our teachers.

KEY 7. RELAX AND LET GO!

SECTION 3. EASY DOES IT!

Mystics long ago spoke of "attachment in detachment"

It is good to detach yourself from people, places and things for a while, because you are apt to take yourself, other people and life in general too seriously.

Without detachment you become too concerned, too tense and when this happens your attention and inner forces flow outward and dissipate. As a result you become tense, rigid and you lose your balance. This tension can become a habit, but when you deliberately practice detachment and relax your grasp, your inner forces are reconnected with your source. You then function at a higher rate of vibration and all the good things of life flow to you instead of away from you.

Many people who are really working on themselves and wanting good results often do their mental and spiritual work under strain. They are invariably anxious or tense and rarely relaxed. AS A RESULT THEY GENERATE IN-HARMONIOUS ENERGY WHICH ACTS AS AN IN-VISIBLE WALL AROUND THEMSELVES WHICH PREVENTS THEM FROM DEMONSTRATING THE VERY THINGS THEY DESIRE AND WORK AND STRAIN SO HARD FOR.

We try to bring our desires into being by our will power. We think we can force things into being. This is the misuse of the will, we are really being wilful. We can do nothing by force for that is going against the nature of things.

Easy does it! When you feel all the work you have done has not been successful then perhaps you are trying too hard. How hard do you work at your affirmations etc? It might help at this stage to give some thought as to how you work at all this. Are you forcing yourself to do all these things and yet feel you are getting nowhere. From the day we are born we are surrounded by people who have been brought up to 'try hard' at whatever it is they have to do. The same pattern is very soon in our own minds. Parents, grandparents—teachers, all in their own way, urged us to 'try hard', whether we wanted to or not.

Children do not understand really what 'try hard' means. If they enjoy doing something, then they will put their hearts and souls into the doing of it and there is no need to urge them on.

If they do not like what they are doing, they do it reluctantly under pressure.

Our society is geared to the 'try hard' syndrome. Hard work gets you everything. Layabouts get nowhere.

So, at an early age we begin to conform, to fit into the pattern. What else can we do?

This is really going against our true nature. Resentment begins when we are forced to 'try hard' at something we are not interested in, but there seems no way out.

At a certain age, most people give up trying and settle for a mediocre existence. The result of this is a feeling of guilt. So we make excuses for not trying. This makes things worse and we become anxious and worried and this causes tension. This in turn causes stress and stress is a killer.

So, we must learn how to overcome tension before it reaches the stress level. Tension is a tightening up. The opposite of this is relaxation which is letting go.

There are many minute tensions of which we are totally unaware. If these are not dealt with they soon lead to major tension and then stress. At the end of this section is a list containing most minute tensions of which we are unaware. Study this and check yourself to see which are yours.

RELAXATION.

The word relax means "to loosen" and "to release". We need to loosen and release our problems so that they can be resolved.

You also need to know how to release and loosen your mind and body.

When you are relaxed you become open and receptive to the power of the universe to flow in and through you.

The simplest method of relaxation costs nothing but a little time each day and practice. Many people say this is too simple to work, but thousands of students are proving that it is very powerful for health and a release from nervous strain, as well as a means of solving problems.

To relax your mind and body you do what comes naturally' by turning within.

First. Sit in a comfortable chair, with your feet slightly apart and your hands resting in your lap, palms down. Make sure that your spine is straight and resting against the chair back. Close your eyes.

Second. Take a deep breath, deep to the bottom of your lungs, then hold it as long as you comfortably can, then slowly exhale. Do this three times then breathe normally.

That is the preparation for relaxation. Practise this a few times so that you know what to do without having to look it up each time it is mentioned.

This preparation is essential and should not be overlooked. When you relax your mind and body and turn within yourself you tune in to the magnetic current of the universe. This magnetic or cosmic current of the universe pulsates through you and about you unceasingly as it does throughout the universe. There is no place where it is absent. You are not aware of this at all but when you relax and get still and turn within, you experience the stillness and peace of this tremendous vibratory energy.

There is no limit to what you can achieve when you relax and become attuned to this magnetic energy in you and around you. It is always there, just waiting for you to contact It.

The Buddha taught that through using this current a man could become so peaceful nothing would ever hurt him. Confucius said that man would never say or do unkind things by tapping the God-force.

Jesus described it as, "the Kingdom of God within you." Paul thought of it as, "Christ in you the hope of glory." Modern scientists call it, electrical energy, innate intelligence and as an atomic vibration of light that fills every cell of man's being. Mystics call it the "white light of spirit,"

Traditional churchmen refer to it as the "Holy Spirit" or "Holy Ghost."

No matter what name you give it, this magnetic current may be contacted and released through relaxation.

Through deep breathing and relaxation of mind and body you tune in to this magnetic current which flows through you, within you and around you. Through regular practice you can attune yourself to the magnetic forces of the universe, which will renew, inspire and uplift you in mind, body and affairs.

You will find an inner stillness you have never known before, which contains all the power, energy and guidance you will ever need.

TEST ON TENSIONS

You must be on your guard constantly against the onset of tension. To refresh your memory, decide whether each of the items in the following list is a symptom of tension or of relaxation:

1. biting nails	tension
2. drinking coffee constantly	tension
3. trembling	tension
4. self-confidence	relaxation
5. yawning	relaxation
6. biting lips	tension
7. critizing others	tension
8. stretching	relaxation
9. indigestion	tension

10. fidgeting	tension
11. ability to wait patiently	relaxation
12. irritability	tension
13. headaches	tension
14. smiling	relaxation
15. skin rashes	tension
16. calmness	relaxation
17. feeling of guilt	tension
18. inability to concentrate	tension
19. eating slowly	relaxation
20. insomnia	tension
21. chain smoking	tension
22. fear of wasting time	tension
23. ability to express a controversial opinion in public.	relaxation
24. excessive perspiration	tension
25. drumming with your fingers	tension
26. scowling	tension

KEY 7. RELAX AND LET GO!

SECTION 4. TUNE IN!

The body is the third part of the trinity of spirit, soul and body. Your body is very important. It is the house in which you live!

"Your body is the temple of the living God."

Without your body you would be unable to function in this finite world. It is your vehicle, or your space-suit, depending upon how you view your existence here at this moment in time.

Every part of your body is important and it should be treated as though it is. I have worked with quite a few people over the years who felt that the sex organs and the organs of elimination were "unclean" or "disgusting". After much work on this kind of attitude they saw quite clearly that it was a carry over from childhood. They had been physically or sexually abused or told that touching the genitals was filthy. Frightening things happen to children which they carry into later life and which destroys all chance of happiness and fulfilment.

A frightened child becomes a frightened adult who will in turn frighten children. A pattern is always repeated unless something is done to change this.

Love your body, every tiny bit of it. Know that you are wonderously made. From the top of your head to the tips of your toes, is sacred.

Once you know the reality of this you will treat your body with great respect.

You will not: stuff yourself with food or eat unwholesome food; pour alcohol endlessly down your throat just to deaden the feelings you cannot face; you will not leave your hair body and clothes unwashed; you will not sit back and watch TV instead of taking regular exercise.

YOU WILL RESPECT YOUR BODY.

Your body is an instrument of the universal life force. If your body and mind are tense then this creative life force is stifled and there is no way it can manifest the good you want in your life. So we must relax the body and mind before we can achieve results.

Your body is an instrument of the mind which enables you to live on this earth plane. It is like a child, it needs constant praise and encouragement. It needs appreciation. It is always ready to receive your mental instructions. When you try to push and force the body to do your will, it causes tension and pain. When you praise, and encourage the body there is relaxation and cooperation from it.

Relaxation of the body means that you have control over it and with this relaxed control you are able to go to deeper levels of meditation.

Sometimes our mind becomes so anxious about what it wants to do that the body is neglected. So we start first with the body. We tell it to relax. We simply say to our body, "relax and let go." Then we expect our body to obey us. Remember, it is like a child and in time it will readily obey our instruction.

EXERCISE Sit down as instructed previously and breathe deeply. with eyes closed. Now focus your attention deep inside your body, from the heart to the navel is the area to choose. As you focus on this area say mentally to your body, "you are wonderful, I love you, I want the very best for you, so just relax and let go." Keep repeating relax and let go as often as you can. Do this gently, remember you are dealing with a child that you are training. It will respond to praise and love and encouragement. Through repetition you will find that your body does relax and feel limp or heavy. That is good and you should tell your body so. Praise it!.

Throughout the day or night, if you feel tense, simply repeat mentally, "relax and let go." You will be reinforcing what you are doing in your relaxation periods. If you find yourself losing control, say it over and over again until you feel calmer.

Once we are able to relax our body then we turn our attention within ourselves and sit quietly waiting in silence. This is not always easy to do as extraneous thoughts flit in and out of our mind. That is fine, so long as we let the thoughts drift out again. **Do not dwell on any thought which comes in meditation.** This will distract us from the purpose of the meditation. Simply acknowledge the thought and then let it go. Too often negative thoughts creep in and we find ourselves dwelling on them. This can be disastrous.

When you sit quietly with your eyes closed you slow down your brain wave cycles and you are at the alpha level of consciousness. At this level you are in touch with your SCM and what you dwell on at this level goes very quickly into your SCM and it is acted upon.

You are vulnerable at this stage and you must guard against any disturbances from outside also. Lock your door, put a sign up, 'do not disturb', take the phone off the hook, make sure that you are not disturbed. This is very important in the early stages. Once you are able to relax at will you will not be disturbed by anything.

A problem remains a problem because of the fierce, tense, possessive hold we have on it.

If this problem intrudes into our relaxation period then we mentally say to it, "I relax and I release you and I let you go. I free you to the perfect solution."

We become very emotionally attached to our problems and can be reluctant to let them go. For our own peace of mind we give them to a Higher Power, within us.

DEEP BREATHING. The way we breathe is very important. Socrates and most ancient Greeks believed that there was a creative or ruling spirit within man which they called the 'breath'. The word breath and the word spirit have the same root meaning in all languages. It is through the breath that you make contact with the spirit. The Greeks saw man as a breath-being, and any illness was diagnosed as a disturbance of his spirit in his breath. They advised people to breathe outward, to empty their lungs entirely of breath, and then draw in the breath with some positive affirmation of good. When they breathed outward again they had only a healing breath going through their bodies and affairs. They also believed that your breath was vitally connected with your happiness. That all despondency and depression could be overcome by breathing in and out words of praise.

So, when you speak words of relaxation to your mind and. body and then deliberately breathe deeply, you unite your spirit., soul and body. You unite your CM your SCM, and your SPCM. (Superconscious mind).

Regular deep breathing is very beneficial. First thing in the morning and last thing at night you should take three deep breaths either out of doors or near an open window. You not only fill your lungs with oxygen but also with the spirit (life forces) outside.

Regular deep breathing will strengthen the delicate tissue of the lungs. The entire heart-lung area will respond with a light, peaceful feeling and your complexion will improve tremendously.

Normally we are shallow breathers, only breathing from the top of the lungs. Deep breathing, sometimes as deep as the abdomen, will improve the blood circulation, give stronger resistance to colds etc and generally promote a wonderful feeling of well-being. You will begin to crave fresh air and will automatically get outside as often as you can. Deep breathing revitalises you very quickly and restores your equilibrium.

EASY DOES IT! When you start the relaxation exercise, remember that there should be no determination to do it. Relaxation is letting go. You are letting go of your body by mentally telling it to relax and let go. As you tell it to relax then you expect it to obey you and relax. The key word is expect. Do not get anxious if at first you are not able to relax. Practice makes perfect. Do it in short sittings.

We then let go of our problems. A good way to stop thoughts from flitting in and out of the mind is to mentally say the word "PEACE" over and over again until you feel peaceful. Again, be careful that you do not get anxious over this. It is all very gentle.

Deep breathing is essential, particularly as you first start the relaxation exercise. Go within yourself. Focus your attention on the heart navel area as this is the SCM area. Just wait in silence for a few moments and then give thanks and open your eyes.

There will be a feeling of peace and well-being after the relaxation.

RELAXATION IS LETTING GO OF YOUR MIND, BODY AND AFFAIRS AND FEELING PEACEFUL AND REFRESHED.

QUESTIONS.

1. Why is it important to have a quiet mind?

2. What has the eye to do with a quiet mind?

3. How can you turn off tense emotions?

4. What is trouble?

5. Which two ways of reacting to problems are compatible with success?

6. How do we prevent over-reacting?

7. What is anger?

8. What is the greatest remedy for anger?

9. Why is it good to detach yourself from people and situations for a while?

10. What is tension?

11. What is relaxation?

12. Why is your body very important?

Do the relaxation exercise regularly, but only for a few minutes at a time. When you can fully relax your body and your mind you will be able to go within yourself and feel the peace that passes understanding.

Peace be still.

SUNSPOTS

**TRY TO KEEP A STIFF
UPPER LIP— EVEN
WHEN THE REST OF
YOUR BODY FEELS LIKE
SAGGING!**

KEY 8. ORDER! ORDER!

SECTION 1. IT'S EVERYWHERE

We live in an orderly universe, in fact order is the first law of the universe. The stars follow an orderly course, the planets revolve around the sun in an orderly way. In nature there is an order of birth, growth, fruition and resting. The seasons come and go with splendid regularity. The sun rises and sets and the moon waxes and wanes all in order. In man there is an orderly pattern of growth. All this order denotes an Infinite Intelligence behind it all. It did not just happen.

Thinking people are able to see clear evidence of a Cosmic Intelligence at work throughout the universe.

Einstein said that there was indisputable evidence of laws of order in the universe. This is also agreed by leading physicists.

What is the evidence for saying this?

MATTER: The way particles of matter are drawn to each other or are repelled by each other shows an orderly intelligence working through law.

CHEMISTRY: The whole science of chemistry is based on the working of this orderly intelligence, which never deviates.

Every blade of grass, every plant or tree that grows is built according to an orderly plan. Without a guiding, creative intelligence to keep the stars and planets on their courses there would be absolute chaos. Our vital organs, heart, stomach, our glands, nerves and blood vessels are constructed according to an orderly plan and it is no accident that they are the same in all human beings. What is our relationship to this universal intelligence?

Science has discovered that all matter is one and that all intelligence is one. And all the so-called laws of the universe are indeed, one law. The intelligence that man uses to dig his garden and plant his seeds is the same intelligence that grows the seeds and runs the universe. The difference is in degree not in kind. We may not fully understand this truth, but the fact is, that whenever we think we think with the one mind of the universe. There is no such thing as 'your' mind and 'my' mind, What we call individual mind is simply that much of the universal mind that we are using at the time.

There is no such thing as 'your' air and 'my' air. there is only one air which is distributed equally around our planet. What I call 'my' air is only that much of the surrounding air that I have drawn into my lungs at the moment. It can be drawn into someone else's lungs and become 'his' or 'hers'.

The real secret of success in anything is in our ability to consciously unite with this universal intelligence and use it to help us remove the negative thought patterns and substitute positive thought patterns in our mind.

Once we can understand that the universal mind fills the universe, we can then imagine it as a great invisible sea of mind surrounding us and in which we are submerged and upon which we can draw whenever we wish.

Let's try and explain this further. A distinguished astrophysicist Sir James Jeans said,

"the universe can best be pictured as consisting of pure thought, the thought for want of a better word we must describe as a Mathematical Thinker."

Once we accept the fact of the Intelligence of the universe we can better understand It's modus operandi, if we think of Its activities in three phases.

This Intelligence cannot be divided into parts we are simply making distinctions so that we can understand more fully with our finite or limited mind, the Infinite Thinker.

For this purpose we have the Infinite Thinker operating on three vibrations.

First, we have the highest and the least tangible vibration which is Spirit. The Infinite Thinker wishes to create a formed universe. With Spirit to wish is to create. Within Spirit is the great, unformed Substance out of which all things are created.

This substance is inert, it must be acted upon by a force outside Itself. It is of the lowest, most tangible vibration.

Spirit uses Mind operating as law to mould and form the universe into the dense material we know.

Mind is the middle vibration. It is lower than Spirit but higher than Matter. So, Spirit, the FIRST PHASE speaks Its will and Mind, the SECOND PHASE, obeys unquestioningly as Law to mould Unformed Substance, the THIRD PHASE, into the form of the pattern that Spirit holds.

The three aspects of the human thinker.

We are also spirit, mind and body.

We are material in our body, so we are one with the Infinite Thinker on the lower vibration, the third phase.

We have a subjective or SCM which makes us one with Spirit on the second level of vibration, or the second phase.

We are thinkers which makes us one with Spirit on the highest vibration, the first phase.

Body. Our body is made of the unformed substance, which is the raw material of the universe. Our body is Spiritual substance but it is of a lower vibration and much more dense than Spirit or Mind. Our body then should not be considered an ugly or blemished thing, but rather a sacred temple in which Spirit dwells. If we can grasp this truth clearly then we can better understand how to heal ourselves.

Mind. Our mind has two phases, the CM and the SCM.

Conscious Mind.

This aspect of our mind is objective. It is reasoning, choosing, directing mind. It corresponds to Spirit in the Infinite Thinker. Man's conscious thinking is not perfect, far from it, but he is spirit in that he has the power and the ability to reason, select and direct subjective mind SCM into the channel that he decides.

Subconscious Mind.

When we are asleep the conscious mind (CM) stops its activities of choosing, reasoning, selecting etc. The SCM however never sleeps. It is constantly working at keeping us functioning as human beings. In that great, unconscious depth are stored memories of past thought and action. These float up in dreams and complexes.

However, this great SCM is more than what has been put into it. It is one with the great, surrounding sea of Mind, which Ralph Waldo Emerson called the Over Soul. Subjective or SCM is creative. The reason it can create new cells and keep us functioning perfectly is because it is in reality one with the Universal Subjective Mind.

Once we understand that there is only one mind in the universe and man is in and of that Mind, we can see that the Mind that made the body cells in the first place can just as easily make new cells impregnated with the picture of perfect health. Universal Subjective Mind always builds according to the pattern laid down by Spirit. Once we recognise that we are spirit and can speak the word that directs Mind to follow that particular pattern, we can set that Law of Mind in action as we want it.

e.g. If we decide that we want to get up at an earlier time than we are used to arising, we make a conscious choice to get up earlier and by picturing the clock at that particular time as we drift off to sleep, we will wake up at precisely that time.

This happens because man as spirit or objective mind, has a servant, subjective mind, which obeys his conscious choice. So, your SCM is the servant of your CM.

One of the most difficult things to grasp by some people is that Universal Mind, with all the powers of the Infinite Thinker, is willing to be the servant of man and flow in the direction that he chooses. If we can remember that this mighty, creative Power is not a person but a principle, the fundamental Principle of the universe, we can understand and use it without any feeling of awe or superstition,

It is a natural law. It is impersonal. It has no more self-consciousness than the law of electricity. It is entirely neutral. It is ready and waiting for man to use It. It never offers or forces Its services, It just awaits recognition. We do not have to pray to it, plead with It, we just have to recognise that It is within us and that It obeys our every thought and feeling.

172

If we keep our thoughts positive and constructive we are giving our servant, our SCM, the right kind of instructions and good things result. If our thoughts are negative and destructive we are giving these instructions to our servant, our SCM and the results are far from pleasant.

We have freedom of choice, we are free to choose the kind of thoughts we wish. If our choice is negative and destructive then it is our own fault if the results are disastrous. No one can do our thinking for us; no one forces us to think and say anything; we make our own decisions. Neither God, nor anyone else sends calamities to us. We bring about our own misfortunes.

We are talking about the law of cause and effect.

We think. This thinking causes something to happen, the effect of that thinking.

Our misfortunes are caused by our own wrong thinking. Remember, if our thinking is resentful, critical and unloving, we feel the effect of that thinking in our own body and affairs. Mean thinking brings mean results. Good, positive thinking brings about good, positive things in our own mind, body and affairs. Wrong thinking cannot hurt the person we are resenting, it can only hurt us.

It is our own responsibility to keep our thoughts good and positive. Students sometimes say they cannot help thinking and feeling resentful about certain happenings. After discussion we find that there is always an underlying cause for the irritation and that is what they have to work on. For example, my Bronchitis experience. See KEY 9, SECTION 2, JUDGE AND JURY.

Wrong thinking means you are out of order, you are not in tune with the creative power of the universe. Nothing will run smoothly unless it is in order and we are responsible for the disorder in our own lives. No other person, no set of circumstances is responsible for the lack of order in our lives. We are solely responsible and this is something we must accept if we wish to be healthy, prosperous, happy and live an abundant life.

I told you at the beginning this was a serious work book. It means you must work at all the exercises diligently before you can feel the wonderful benefit of it all. But work with a light heart and enjoy it. It has changed my life and the lives of my students and it can change yours also, if you let it.

Spend extra time with this lesson for there is a lot to digest here. It will take many readings and some meditation to find the truth of it all.

It will be time well spent.

KEY 8. ORDER! ORDER!

SECTION 2. LAW AND ORDER.

For any society to function efficiently there must be a system of law and order. If man was left entirely to his own devices the result would be chaos. The greed and selfishness, the hatred and resentment towards his fellow man would burst forth like a spent up fury and would, not only destroy the environment and habitat, but even mankind itself. Laws are necessary in our society as a means of protecting man against man.

It is true that not everyone obeys the laws of the land, but the offenders are in a minority and they have to be deterred under the law. We are all at different levels of development and what one person sees as his right another sees as a crime.

Man in his ignorance of the one law seeks outside himself for what he needs. Outer things are not permanent they pass away. When you buy a new car for example, it will eventually break down and rust away. As new models are built old ones are discarded. Man is forever seeking perfection without realising that perfection is found first within himself. All the so-called good things of life, the beautiful home, the fastest car, the designer clothes, the best of everything, only come as the result of the inner awareness of how we function as human beings and our purpose in being here.

Simply put, the thinking, the beliefs and attitudes we hold about ourselves and other people become a reality in our lives and we have fastened them there. We may be obedient to the laws of society but are we obedient to the inner law of our being? In common language, our conscience is the inner law we should obey. But how many people are aware they have a conscience?

Order is not something we frantically rush around doing trying desperately to put things right.

Order is a mental power or faculty, one of twelve, which is located at a large ganglionic nerve centre in the solar plexus area, behind the navel. Despair, fear, sickness and weakness particularly in this solar plexus area is a sign that things are out of order in your life and affairs. On the other hand, health, freedom and peace of mind are yours when your mental power of order is functioning correctly. Negative thoughts and emotions dam up the creative life force within and this stops the body from renewing itself. As a result there is disease and discomfort in every aspect of life.

Order works through emotional harmony. If a certain kind of order is achieved without harmonious agreement there will be confusion because this is not order but conflict as one person gets the better of another through force, double dealing or dishonesty. Disharmony or inharmonious means "something is out of order" and whether the inharmonious condition is in your mind, body or affairs, the only way to have harmony is to develop and use your mind power of order.

Order begins within. A chief executive I know, a very efficient man, was faced with a problem he felt he could not control. Everything seemed to be getting out of hand. He could not attend our classes so he asked me to visit him at work during his lunch break. I was shown into his large office and given coffee. As he talked he seemed taut and highly strung. His face reflected strain which had not been there three years ago when I first met him. "The day is not long enough for all the things I have to do," he said, almost, it seemed, in despair. I looked at his desk, a very large one, it was cluttered. He waved his hand over it all as though he did not know how to get rid of it all and hoped I would wave a magic wand and make it disappear.

It was obvious that his affairs were anything but orderly. He blamed others for things that were going wrong. It was not just his desk but his colleagues, his wife and family and the powers that be.

Perfect order is in my mind, body and affairs now and all is well!

This was the affirmation he used, repeating it over and over as often as he could, no matter where he was.

The next step was to arrive at his office half an hour earlier each morning and sit at his desk with a blank sheet of paper before him. He then had to close his eyes and focus his attention on the solar plexus area, behind his navel which is in the SCM area. He then had to say to his inner self, his SCM

The work that I do today is in line with the order of the universe, no matter what I believe about it.

He had to repeat this with great feeling fifteen times. He then gave thanks to his SCM. He was in fact giving orders to his faithful servant, his SCM. Then he had to make a list of all the important things he had to do that day. He then had to rewrite the list in order of importance after a brief reflection. During the day he had to work from the top of the list downwards until all were completed. As he completed each task he crossed it out and did the next one. It did not matter if some days he did not finish the list, the remaining ones headed his list the next day.

He found it took great discipline to do this as he was frequently tempted to skip through the list at random, or he was tempted to tackle anything that came up unexpectedly. He said he tended to make the excuse that the new thing was urgent and should be dealt with right away. He overcame this by actually stopping what he was doing and relaxing and saying the affirmation for a while. He was then able to rationalise to himself about the new task. "If I was away then this particular thing would have to wait until I returned", he said to himself and other such things. He was determined to get back to his usual cheerful, happy self. I had a phone call whenever he felt he might weaken, but after that he certainly used his will-power very successfully to keep himself doing the things on his list.

Weeks later he took me out to lunch and gave me a large cheque. He found that when he stuck to his lists things were done so efficiently and quickly it almost took his breath away. He still uses the affirmations for every aspect of his life and he has regained his old confidence and is highly successful and he even has time to spare! When he reminded himself that order was in the universe and always will be, he began to see that the lack of order in his own life was through his own attitudes and emotions. The more he tried to change other people and events in an outer way only made them worse and he became more and more depressed.

The tremendous, creative power of the universe is within us. It only awaits our recognition so we can use it for a better and more successful life. This power is contacted through the use of the law of Mind. We are constantly using the Law of Mind though we may not be aware of it.

The law of mind is the law of belief.

What do you believe? Every thought you have, if it is held constantly and with feeling, becomes a habit and this habit is your belief.

It is as simple as that!

Think and feel often enough about one thing and you have your belief.

As children we were taught to clean our teeth regularly. We repeated this action until, over the years, it became a habit, an automatic action. We no longer think about it we just do it. Whatever you think and feel to be true, will be impressed in your SCM and it will come to pass. This applies whether the thoughts and feelings are good or bad, it is the law—the law of your being. Your dominant conviction about yourself controls all lesser thoughts, ideas, actions and reactions. If your dominant conviction is:

The order of the universe is in my mind, body and affairs now, it will sink down into your deeper mind and become a habit.

"According to your faith let it be done unto you."

(Matt, 9:29)

This does not say according to your Protestant, Catholic., Jewish, Hindu or Buddhist faith. NO! It simply means it is done to you according to your faith, your belief, in the creative laws of your own mind, which you can learn and apply to every aspect of your life. The electrician learns the laws and principles of electricity and the mathematician learns the principles and laws of mathematics.

Life is a principle. Learn all you can about it and use the

principle wisely. You cannot dodge, hide or escape from the laws of your mind. The Universal Intelligence is no respecter of persons and plays no favourites. The law of life is one of absolute progression. We progress from one experience to another. What we learn from each experience depends on our state of mind at the time. There is always something to learn from the greatest disaster for there is order in everything.

Think of a tree. Its roots go deep into the ground and extract the necessary chemicals and moisture from the soil for its growth and unfoldment. You are like that tree. Your real roots are deep in the Universal Intelligence and you can extract from this Source of all, inspiration, guidance, prosperity, power, wealth and anything you need to lead a full and happy life. There is a subjective wisdom in the roots of the tree which enables it to suck up all the water needed for nourishment. You also can be refreshed, rejuvenated by allowing your thoughts to dwell on the Living Intelligence within you to guide you, inspire you and vitalise your whole being.

Remember the subjective area, your SCM, is in the region of the body from the heart to the navel. Close your eyes and visualise this part of you as the place where Creative Intelligence resides. Feel the Presence there, talk to this Intelligence mentally as you sit relaxed and at ease. Always say things that are good and positive and speak as though you already have the desired thing. "Thank you for the perfect healing now."

"Thank you for my perfect work now."

"Thank you for guiding me to my right place in life."

"Thank you for my perfect wealth."

Just give thanks and speak as though the thing you wanted has already appeared. Also visualise it as being already in your possession.

You are talking to your obedient servant, your SCM, the law or principle of life within you.

KEY 8. ORDER! ORDER!

SECTION 3. OUT OF ORDER!

The faculty of order is located in the solar plexus area behind the navel. It is in the SCM area the subjective area, the feeling, emotional area. This fact indicates that it is first an emotional quality.

The ancients called this centre behind the navel the "lyden gland." Many great mystics and philosophers throughout the ages refer to this important gland as the order centre in man.

If one is out of order then one looks for the emotional cause.

The term, "You are out of order," is frequently used when someone has overstepped the mark, or when one has disregarded the general consensus of opinion. If we are aggressive we are out of order; if we criticise we are out of order; if we 'do someone down' we are out of order; in fact, if we do anything to upset others in any way we are out of order.

A child has a tantrum, he is out of order; if we have a stomach upset, we are out of order; if we are broke, we are out of order.

In other words, every time we are not happy, prosperous, fulfilled human beings we are out of order and the root cause of it is due to our emotions.

Order works through emotional harmony within ourselves.

Many people try to impose order by force. This never works it only causes confusion and chaos.

Throughout history dictators have lost their power and their lives through trying to impose order by force.

I once worked in a school where the male members of staff were trying to get Boxing on the curriculum. The female staff were totally opposed to the idea as they felt it was brutish and inhuman and could cause problems to the health of the children. In particular they were thinking of brain damage. The sports teachers made out a very good case for Boxing as a sport which helps self reliance. One thing in particular caught my interest. They said that any good, well-trained Boxer knew how to keep his emotions under control, that a Boxer could never defeat his opponent if he got mad. He would lose control and as a result would hit out in blind fury, forgetting all the good techniques he had learned and as a result would fail.

How many times do we lose our temper over trivial things, over things that are unimportant? Why do we do it? When someone treats us unfairly, lies about us, cheats us, how do we react? We get angry and upset, we are out of order. Whenever we get mad we cloud our judgement, and as a result we do something foolish, or seemingly insane and even tragic or fatal things. We lose the control that we normally have in our day to day existence.

As a parent and as a teacher of teenagers I have often been faced with the kids who will always "talk back" or refuse to do what they are asked to do.

I can say this, it is always easier to handle other people's children than one's own in times of stress.

One is so used to living with one's own children it comes as quite a shock when there is a refusal to obey. I felt in one instance my elder daughter was being totally unreasonable and I said so.

That was a mistake. She had been upset at school and was still smarting under the hurt feelings caused by her friend's disloyalty, so shouting at me and refusing to do as she was asked was a release of pent up anger and hurt. She was completely out of control emotionally so I turned on my heel and left the room. I had to get away from the scene for I could feel my anger starting to rise and I knew it would make matters worse. When my daughter finally came downstairs she sheepishly said, "sorry", and sat down and joined me in a cup of tea. It was then I learned of her upset at school, the reason for the eruption of her hurt and angry feelings.

When dealing with a class of children there is total impartiality, there is no emotional involvement as there is with one's own children. This does not mean that teachers do not care about the people they teach, on the contrary, I cared very much about each of them as individuals. I liked them and they knew it, but I also saw the individual potential of each student and used that accordingly. I recognised their talents and also their weaknesses and we worked together to bring forth the abilities the child often did not realise he had.

I was impartial and I made sure the rules I set were obeyed or they suffered the consequences. The rules were simple.

1. I would not accept rudeness from anyone, because I would never be rude to them. If I ever was rude, then they had my permission to be rude back, for I would have deserved it.

2. I enjoyed my work and liked to work in a happy atmosphere. My work was teaching them and I expected them to work as hard as I did. Working together was a much better framework for cooperation than just telling them to do something because I said so.

They all loved and respected me and they all worked their little butts off for me. The secret is really praise, encouragement and appreciation. I showed good manners to them and they responded with good manners. They also knew that any problem they had could be sorted out by me so crises did not arise.

We had a framework of order.

In Physics they were taught the laws of cause and effect and I showed them how to apply this knowledge to their everyday situations. This went a great way to solving problems and not laying blame.

When you get mad and do something silly in anger, it is not the deed you do that matters so much as giving up the responsibility of your life to your emotions instead of to your intelligence.

Everything works in order through the Law of the universe. And Law is always good, it cannot be anything else. If we break the Law we are misusing It and we suffer the consequences. Have you ever lost something important to you such as your door key, your purse or wallet, an important paper or a keepsake? How did you react? Was your first reaction PANIC? From then on did you frantically rush around trying to find it and visualising all kinds of negative things happening because of the apparent loss?

Instead of rushing around, which only enhances the loss, the first thing to do on discovering something is missing is to take three deep breaths. This will give you a time to calm down and think logically.

When was the last time you had this missing item in your possession? Think about it. Try and remember all the details about the last time you had it in your hands. Keep calm as you do this and sit down for a while. Mentally go over the scene before its disappearance. Recall as many details as you can. Keep this up for a time until you feel you have exhausted all possibilities then give it to your SCM to find. Get up and make yourself busy. Do not think about the loss again. Just rest assured that your wonderful SCM will find it for you. Say an affirmation such as,

My SCM knows where ... is and it shows me now!

The next thing you do is let go of it and trust your SCM to show you. Trust is the operative word here. Trust your inner self, It knows all the answers.

On the few times I have mislaid something I immediately stop the feeling of annoyance and I actually tell my SCM to show me where it is. I trust It completely and I never doubt. That is the only secret.

A young first year student came rushing into my office just before the bell for morning assembly rang. She was in a panic. She had only been in the school a few weeks and was still unsure of herself.

She had lost her purse which contained her lunch money for the week and also her bus fare home. She began to cry so I sat her down and gave her a tissue to dry her eyes and asked where she had lost it. She didn't know. It was only when she looked in her school bag that she realised it wasn't there. I told her not to worry about her lunch, that I would see the secretary and she could have it as usual. I also told her to ask the secretary for a bus token at the end of the day. She wiped her eyes and smiled and thanked me then went on her way to assembly. I paused for a second and asked my SCM to give me a clue to the whereabouts of the purse.

I then gathered up my things and went to the hall to take assembly. I smiled at the school and told then to sit down. As I looked down at the first row of children the young girl was sat right in front of me. We smiled at each other and then assembly proceeded. As I walked from the hall afterwards to my office I suddenly had the idea to ring the child's mother at home. She was both relieved and excited when I explained about the missing purse.

"Oh, it's here, I found it on the hall table after she had left. I was going to bring it in this morning."

So, we were back to order again.

Disorder of any kind is not the normal, natural way of life. Even children are in disorder when they are excited or anxious about something. This little girl was new to a secondary school where a more adult approach is expected. In her anxiety not to be late or to miss the bus or to forget anything she had put the purse down on the hall table whilst she put on her coat. A simple thing? It is the simple things that upset us so much when we are out of order. Two years later that child was a student to be proud of. She went out of her way to help all the new intake as they came in. A future prefect and later Head Girl. She learned from her own experience and put it to use by helping others.

A lesson for us all!

KEY 8. ORDER! ORDER!

SECTION 4. RUNNING SMOOTHLY.

Order is not a daily routine or a carefully followed set of habits. We can get up at the same time each day, have the same kind of breakfast, go to work by the same route, have a set night for this hobby and a set night and time for that interest. All this is just a daily routine which perhaps started years ago and is now a firm habit, something we do without much thought about it. We feel secure with it and any deviation from it aggravates and frustrates us. WE DO NOT LIKE TO CHANGE THIS COMFORTABLE, SAFE WAY OF LIVING THAT WE HAVE FIRMLY ESTAB-LISHED FOR OURSELVES.

But change we must if we are to survive for this is not order it is stagnation.

Order is not the outer appearance of a regular routine. It is the perfect balance which is achieved in our lives and cir-cumstances when we work with the law of being, within ourselves.

Order, real order is achieved when we put first things first. It is the inner balance of mind and heart, the intellect and the emotions.

We are frequently caught up in a struggle between mind and heart, we are ruled either by our intellect or our emo-tions. Think of the times when your emotions have been so powerful that you felt it was right to go ahead with the feel-ings you had. Suddenly you were confronted with thoughts that dictated to you, 'there is no way you can do these things'. You were in a turmoil.

Sometimes the emotions are so strong they override the thoughts, on other occasions the limiting thoughts take over. It does not matter whether the intellect or the emo-tions sway us in our decision making, either way the results are far from pleasing nor are they successful.

Neither the intellect nor the emotions are right. We must have balance, a harmonious working together of emotions and intellect if we are to be peaceful, happy, prosperous and fulfilled.

Both our thoughts and feelings are of equal importance and they are both valid. Do not despise your feelings because they get you into many involvements which you regret. Do not worship your intellect as it passes cool judgement, often without mercy, on people and circumstances.

Many great intellectual thinkers can be emotionless and as a result they do not have good personal relationships. A great many people are ruled totally by their emotions and lead lives of misery, rejection and early death. Our thoughts and feelings are of equal importance and neither should dominate.

Deep within the centre of your being is a place that is always peaceful and calm. Nothing can disturb it. It is rather like the hub of a wheel which remains still even when the wheel is turning. In times of stress take a minute to relax in a quiet place undisturbed. Close your eyes and focus your attention on the heart navel area. Just mentally say the words, "Peace be still". Repeat these words silently until you feel relaxed and peaceful. Then rest quietly for a moment, then slowly open your eyes, stretch and then get up and go about your business.

Students find that doing this in times of stress gives them a great boost and they are able to cope with anything that confronts them. This is a way of reaching this calm centre. If your emotions are tangled and your body seems unable to relax then doing this exercise will help tremendously. If at first you feel unable to relax don't worry about it. Worry only causes further tension. The aim is to have a calm moment with your inner self, to touch the peace and calm that is deep within yourself.

Once you can accept the great, creative power within your own mind you will be at peace.

To work successfully with this power we must realise we are working with principle or law. So a good, general affirmation will open the way for new ideas and concepts to flow into our mind.

Universal Wisdom is guiding my entire life.

Repeat this as often as you can, write it down also. At this stage you should know what you desire most in your life. Are you any nearer towards achieving that desire? If not, it could be that you are either, trying too hard, "I'll do it if it kills me," attitude towards it.

Or, are you being too specific? 'I want a specific job' rather than, completely, satisfying work?

Do you want a specific 'deal' or, constantly increasing success?

Do you want your own way in an argument, or, the harmonious solution of it?

It is not wise to be too specific at the present level of development.

Do we fully understand the implications of what we demand? Are we wise enough yet? We cannot really see far enough into the future to be sure that what we presently desire will bring all the happiness and success we feel it can.

Always insisting on having our own way whether right or not is rather like a stubborn child insisting on having his own way. Like Ben aged seven who was having a painting session on the kitchen table. His mother told him to pack up as it was lunch time and she needed the table. Ben said, "no", and carried on painting. Again he was asked and again he refused. This time his mother very firmly said pack up or else. Ben reluctantly began to collect his things together. In his resentment at being forced to do something he did not want to do, he pulled sharply at the paper underneath his painting and upset the water all over the table and himself.

"That was a stupid thing to do," said his mother. Immediately Ben banged his fist down on the table and shouted, "I am not stupid." In a stern voice his mother said, "I did not call you stupid, I said it was a stupid thing to do, and it was. Go up to your room." Ben flounced out. Ten minutes later he came downstairs and said in a sheepish voice, "You're right, it was a stupid thing to do, I'm sorry." He cleaned everything up beautifully.

We can be very childish in our insistence that everything

must be as we want it to be no matter what. We refuse to compromise, to see the other side of things. Our insistence can bring us a great deal of trouble and strife and disorder.

The desire we wish to attain may not be a big enough desire nor comprehensive enough for our good. If however, we think about and work with the fundamental principles of success instead of specific things, we will not only be more successful but we will find a bigger and more valuable achievement.

The positive fundamentals of success are, a perfect home, a perfect love relationship, abundance, congenial work, joy, happiness, fulfilment etc. We can ask our SCM to guide us to our perfect work for instance.

I have a perfect work in a perfect way, I give a perfect service for perfect pay!

This is a fundamental affirmation which allows no restrictions to be placed upon it. How do you know what is exactly right for you at the moment. A month later you may change your mind. Or the thing you get may not be all that you thought it would be. You can never see the snags when you are set upon a specific thing.

Please do not misunderstand this. I am not saying you should be wishy-washy about your goals, or just lazily feel you will leave everything in the lap of the gods. Far from it. You have to know you need a home or a job or a mate or money. That is specific enough. Work for a while with the affirmation,

Universal wisdom is guiding my entire life.

Then when you feel a response to this add your affirmation for your desire.

e.g. "UNIVERSAL WISDOM IS GUIDING ME TO MY RIGHT WORK NOW. WITH UNIVERSAL WISDOM I AM SUCCESSFUL IN ALL THAT I DO."

"I HAVE ACCESS TO THE WEALTH OF THE UNIVERSE."

"I AM A CHILD OF THE UNIVERSE AND I SHARE AND EXPERIENCE THE ABUNDANCE AND WEALTH OF CREATION."

You need a perfect home, not a certain house.

You need satisfying work, not a certain job.

You need strong, accumulating success, not a certain deal

What you really want is certain fundamental satisfactions, not specific things.

Make no mistake about this. Once you set your goals in the right way, the fundamental way, your success will be way beyond your wildest dreams.

Your life will flow logically and smoothly, step by step until you reach your ultimate goal. You will then look back in amazement at what you have gained. Something far beyond your comprehension at this moment.

YOU CAN IF YOU THINK YOU CAN!

QUESTIONS.

1. What is the first law of the universe?

2. What evidence have we for thinking there is a Cosmic Intelligence working throughout the universe?

3. What are the three vibrations of the Infinite Thinker?

4. What are the three vibrations of the human thinker?

5. Why are laws necessary in society?

6. What is the inner law of our being?

7. How does order work?

8. What is the law of the universe?

9. What is your obedient servant?

10. What causes us to be 'out of order'?

11. Is order a daily routine?

12. Is it always right to insist on our own way?

SUNSPOTS

**LET ALL THINGS BE
DONE DECENTLY AND
IN ORDER.**
I. Corinthians 14:40

KEY 9. NO REGRETS!

SECTION 1. I CAN'T TURN BACK THE CLOCK!

Most people are filled with regret and remorse over things they did or did not do in the past. Periodically they bring out these ghosts which haunt them and they wallow in the self-pity this brings.

Every human being has done something of which they are ashamed. Mostly these things are minor, but the regrets stimulate the imagination into great activity, so the incident is enlarged out of all proportion. It is as though we have this need to punish ourselves.

Regrets are a waste of time. It is all water under the bridge.

The Past Is Gone.

You can only live in the present, the past is gone.

If you will remember and use this statement as an affirmation you will make a profound change in your life.

You can only live in the present. The past has gone.

You cannot live in the past. You can cherish past joys, and you may not entirely forget past sorrows.

But, these are past events—they are memories, not PRESENT EMOTIONS!

This is most important if you want a happy, successful, prosperous, fulfilled and happy life.

Past joys and past sorrows are **past.** The past is **GONE. SO, CLOSE THE DOOR ON IT!**

You must totally accept the fact that the past has **GONE** The past is memory. Only the present exists.

There is only now!

You may remember the past—as past, but you cannot relive it.

You cannot change the past.

YOU CAN ONLY LIVE IN THE PRESENT!

Your past mistakes are gone with the past. Some of the consequences of the past mistakes may carry over into the present—to be dealt with in the present.

But, your past mistakes are **gone** with. the past.

You cannot relive the event with a second chance to do better!

You can learn from your past mistakes as you would learn from any historical event. But such learning should be intellectual—not emotional. Just as you would study any history!

If you emotionalise memories of past mistakes, griefs and resentments, you add to your difficulties with the present. If you emotionalise memories of past unhappiness you will have greater unhappiness in the present; because your mind is geared to unhappiness by this constant resurrection.

The past is gone, so close the door on it.

Open the door on a present filled with opportunities you can do something about.

Present opportunities are now!

And now is all there really is!

The world belongs to those people who, by a process of elimination, find out what will not work and discover what will work.

Successs is:

1. Finding out what will not work,
and

2. Discovering, by elimination, what will work.

In other words, you have to learn from your own experiences, and this includes your own failures.

Failure is one of the most effective methods you can use to succeed!

Failure should not be feared and avoided; it should be accepted and used.

Learn to fail intelligently.

1. Keep on trying and failing and failing and trying.

2. No matter how often you fail—do not suffer any ego damage because of frequent failures.

Some people, the instant failures, fail a few times and suffer ego damage, so they become discouraged and give up. They are then permanent failures. They panic after a few failures and then withdraw into their shell of nothingness. All because their first few failures hurt their precious egos.

Whilst you must not let failing hurt your ego, neither must you let mistakes nag you with a sense of guilt.

Now, this does not mean you condone "deliberate mistakes", which are not mistakes at all, but are deliberate wrongdoings. It is not intelligent, nor commendable, nor moral, to do what you know, or even believe to be wrong. Deliberate wrongdoing deserves the inevitable sense of guilt which is its certain consequence.

This does not apply to the countless mistakes which are not deliberate wrongdoing, which are the natural consequences of not being perfect—and what human being is?

No one should suffer ego damage or a sense of guilt because of honest mistakes which are the result of the valuable learning process of "testing" to find out what will not work so that, by elimination, ore finally discovers what will work.

These "testing" failures are not deliberately immoral, no sense of guilt is involved. There is instead a sense of achievement, accomplishment, because you will be one step closer to finding what will work.

Thomas Edison spent ten years making "continuing mistakes" before he found the right way to make the storage battery. He and his staff tested and classified 17,000 varieties cf plants before they succeeded in extracting latex in substantial quantities from just one of them!

Edison failed more than anyone else. As a result he knew more things that wouldn't work than anyone else. So, with that kind of information he succeeded more than anyone else. He patented 1,093 inventions worth millions! All this information is well recorded.

IS YOUR FEAR OF MAKING MISTAKES STOPPING YOU FROM BEING A BIG SUCCESS?

KEY 9. NO REGRETS.

SECTION 2. NOT GUILTY!

Guilt is the most destructive, the most useless, the most stagnant of all energies.

People often ask, "How can I deal with something I am ashamed of or sorry for?"

Well, the only way to deal with anything one is ashamed of, is by genuine remorse, not guilt.

Honest remorse springs from the heart and it is a cleanser. True remorse means accepting responsibility for your own actions. It means maturity of character and with it comes the desire to compensate. If this is possible, then compensate the best way you can then let go of the remorse.

If there is no way at the present time of compensating, then forgive yourself and resolve to learn from that experience. There will come a time in the future, when, an opportunity for compensating will arise. Your SCM will attract to you the way and the situation for compensation.

It is highly commendable to accept responsibility for your own actions even if this is painful to you at the time. It shows great maturity and will give you a good feeling of achievement.

In the feeling that your actions have caused another human being pain, is the beginning of a sense of guilt, which should be nipped in the bud immediately.

Guilt is negative and unrealistic. It does not help you or the one who is hurt. It is a useless exercise and means nothing. It glues all things together and there is a sense of suffocation and aloneness and you wonder how on earth you can escape from it.

You are the judge!

You are in the unique position of being both the judge and the jury in your life and experiences. You weigh up all the evidence in connection with any situation or problem, and, after due deliberation, you announce your verdict. The sentence or penalty involved is one that you cannot avoid.

Sometimes it is not even necessary to reach a verdict of

your own, instead you may readily accept those that other people have pronounced for you.

This immediately raises the questions
What are you doing to yourself?
How valid are the verdicts you have reached or accepted?
What kind of a sentence are you serving?
What kind of a penalty are you paying?
How much are you depriving yourself of health, abundance, love, joy, happiness and the other things that make life worth living?

Every waking moment you are reaching a verdict concerning yourself; you are making a decision; you are choosing, deciding what kind of a life you will have.

You can learn to be a better judge. You can discover a way to keep from stacking the jury against yourself. You can find a way to better evaluate the evidence and of the utmost importance, you can learn always to reach a verdict that is in your favour.

I can illustrate this by my own example.

Many years ago, when I first came to live in London, I developed Bronchitis. For two years the pattern of my working life was; three weeks ill, five or six weeks working. This happened with incredible regularity. I was bedfast, given massive doses of penicillin and cough medicine. I became resigned to this pattern of Bronchitis with the medication and bedrest, then work for a few weeks until I had another attack.

This went on for two years! Finally, during a very severe attack, I received a letter from my daughter which said, 'I was in the health shop and for some unknown reason, I was drawn to the book shelf and found myself reaching for this book enclosed. As I wondered what I was doing, the thought came to me to send it to you. I hope this makes sense to you, it doesn't to me!'

The book was Barbara Cartland's book on Honey. I read it, because I felt I should do as my daughter had sent it. I had never been a lover of honey, but my husband bought some and I began to take it instead of the medicine. It eased my cough and my chest felt easier. A few days later, still in bed, I had an awareness that if this illness continued I would die. This disturbed me. I wasn't ready to die yet, but what could I do?

The answer came swiftly from my SCM. Get up and go to the doctor. I did! As I sat waiting for my turn to see him, I wondered what on earth I would say to him, and also what he would say to me.

He was horrified to see me for he knew I had walked from home four blocks away. I told him I wanted the tablets changed, the skin was off my tongue and mouth and I had a permanent headache. I also said that I would not get better until these were changed.

He gently said he would have come to see me as I should not be outside in this condition and yes he would give me a new prescription.

I had two further weeks off work and each day I used positive-affirmations to keep me going and I only stayed in bed for half the first week.

I was determined never to have Bronchitis again and that became my goal. For two years after that I took honey twice a day and also cod liver oil capsules. Bronchitis did not occur. I was cured. Last year however, I got it again after we were flooded out and were without heating for a while. I dosed myself up with honey and cod liver oil and kept my mind right and it went quickly without help from the doctor. It is now on my medical records that I cannot take antibiotics.

Going back to judge and jury.

THE EVIDENCE: Bronchitis.

THE VERDICT: Pain and suffering and a limited experience of living.

First there was the fact that I had Bronchitis. Second, I accepted the verdict that nothing could cure this and I would have recurring bouts all my life. Third, I was serving the sentence I had accepted for myself.

Then there came a time when I discovered that perhaps the evidence had been misinterpreted. This did not mean that I did not have Bronchitis, but rather that behind the evidence, the appearance of the disease, there was something else that had caused it to appear. I knew my own wrong thinking had caused this. I did not want to live in London and I resented the fact that I had been forced to give up my job, which I loved, to move there.

I recognised the ability of life to express Itself in and through me in a normal and natural way which was free from crippling limitation. This was my new verdict which freed me from the previous ones relating to my condition. I was determined to have the good things I desired and these came about.

KEY 9. NO REGRETS.

SECTION 3. ERRORS.

Throughout our life we incur emotional wounds from other people and we inflict them upon ourselves. We beat ourselves over the head with self-condemnation, remorse and regret. We beat ourselves down with self-doubt. We cut ourselves up with excessive guilt.

Remorse and regret are attempts to emotionally live in the past. Excessive guilt is an attempt to make right IN THE PAST something we did wrong or thought of as wrong in the past. Since we cannot live in the past, we cannot react emotionally to the past. The past can simply be written off, closed, forgotten insofar as our emotional reactions are concerned. The important thing is our present direction and our present goal.

We need to recognise our own errors as mistakes. Unless we do this we cannot correct our course, steering or guidance would be impossible. **It is futile and fatal to hate or condemn ourselves for our mistakes.**

In thinking of our mistakes (and those of others) it is helpful and realistic to think of them in terms of what we did or didn't do, rather than in terms of what the mistakes made us.

One of the biggest mistakes we can make is to confuse our behaviour with our "self"...to conclude that because we did a certain act it characterises us as a certain sort of person.

It clarifies our thinking if we can see that mistakes involve something we "do"—our actions, and, if we are realistic we should use verbs denoting action, rather than nouns denoting a state of being, when describing them.

e.g. To say, "I failed", (verb form) is simply recognising an error and this can lead to future success. But to say "I am a failure" (noun form) does not describe what YOU DID, but what YOU THINK THE MISTAKE DID TO YOU.

This does not contribute to learning, it tends to fix the mistake in your mind and make it permanent. This has been proved over and over again in clinical, psychological experiments.

All children when learning to walk will fall down and get up again. We say, "he fell" or "he stumbled". We do not say "he is a stumbler" or "he is a faller".

A great many parents fail to recognise that all children, in learning to talk, also make mistakes. They hesitate, block, repeat words and syllables. Parents assume from what they hear "he is a stutterer".

Such an attitude-a judgement, which is not of the child's actions, but of the child himself, gets across to the child and he begins to think of himself as a stutterer. His learning is fixed and the stutter becomes permanent.

Parents have frequently said to me their child is a stutterer, using a judgemental term, "he could not speak" instead of a descriptive term "he did not speak".

The parents, not the child, were the most in need of understanding and instruction.

BAD HABITS. The above principal applies also to nearly all bad habits, including emotional habits. We have to stop blaming ourselves, condemning ourselves, and feeling remorseful over our habits. That is, if we want to cure them! What is particularly damaging is the verdict, "I am ruined", or, "I am worthless". because I have done, or am doing, certain things.

So, remember, **"You" make mistakes. Mistakes don't make "you"—anything!**

To live creatively we must be willing to be a little vulnerable. We must be willing to be hurt a little—if necessary, in creative living. A lot of people need a thicker and tougher emotional skin than they have. But they need only a tough, emotional skin, not a shell!

To trust, to love, to open ourselves to emotional communication with other people is to run the risk of being hurt. If we are hurt once, we can do one of two things. We can build a thick, protective shell to prevent being hurt again, live like an oyster, and not be hurt. Or we can "turn the other cheek", remain vulnerable and go on living crea- tively.

An oyster is never hurt. He has a thick, protective shell, he is isolated. If a speck of grit gets into the shell he imme- diately secretes a solution which covers the particle of grit and so removes the pain. The oyster is secure, but he is not creative. He cannot go after what he wants, he must wait for it to come to him. An oyster knows none of the hurts of emo- tional communication with his environment, but neither can he know the joys!

All our experiences are learning experiences. If we can accept this, we will then learn tremendous things about ourselves from each of these experiences.

Whatever the problem or situation, start to look for the good in it. Ask yourself, "What can I learn from this?"

If you do this constantly you will find that things improve and your emotions will become more under your control.

An old lady who has been housebound for years said, "What on earth is the world coming to. Where will it all end?" Each day she sits in her room worrying about the troubles of the world. When she was young there was none 'of this trouble', so she says. She watches the news on TV and worries about all 'the goings on'. She suffers severely from Arthritis and is overweight. Few people visit her be- cause her conversation is so depressing. She will not make the effort to change. She is unable to meet the challenges and changes of life, yet she is better looked after than she would have been when she was young! She never ap- preciates the home help who keeps her home clean and fresh, she does not appreciate the nourishing food that is brought to her piping hot from her next door neighbour. There is a library service which comes to her home so she has ample reading material of her own choice. She has many blessings to be thankful for but she always complains.

There are many people who react to problems in a similar way. They are bitter, pessimistic, fearful, anxious and troubled. Every challenging experience that comes to people with this kind of consciousness is regarded as a prob- lem, and problems to them are hopeless situations.

There is no situation that is hopeless. In fact you do not have a problem, only the one that is in your own mind and you put it there! Think about this very carefully. Problems are caused by wrong thinking. We make our own problems by the way we think about any situation that arises or whatever people do to us. There is no situation that is hopeless, that cannot be worked through in a satisfactory way for everyone concerned. It is our responsibility to calm down and look at things in a different way. It is our responsibility to do this, not someone else.

We must accept responsibility for everything that upsets us, for we allow things to upset us! We blame others for errors made then we wonder why we feel hurt and unhappy. Our errors in judgement are made by us and they are stepping stones from which we learn.

KEY 9. NO REGRETS.

SECTION 4. LET GO.

Imagine, if you will, yourself sitting quietly at home reading a book and the telephone rings. Automatically you put your book down, stand up and go and answer it. You did this without thinking about it. You responded to a stimulus. This outside stimulus had the effect of moving you. It changed your mental set and your position or self-determined course of action. You were all set to spend a quiet hour relaxed with a book. You were inwardly organised for this. Now all is changed by your response to the external stimuli.

The point is, you do not have to answer the telephone, you do not have to obey. You can, IF YOU CHOOSE, totally ignore the telephone. You can, if you choose, continue sitting there reading. You can continue to maintain your own, original state of organisation by REFUSING TO RESPOND to the signal.

Get this mental picture clearly in your mind for it can be quite helpful in overcoming the power of external stimuli to disturb you. See yourself sitting there quietly relaxed and letting the phone ring, ignoring its signal, unmoved by its command.

Also get clearly in your mind that the outside signal in itself has no power over you. In the past you have obeyed it, responded to it, simply out of habit. You can, if you choose, form a new habit by not responding.

Notice that your failure to respond does not consist in 'doing something', or making an effort, or resisting, or fighting, but in 'doing nothing', in relaxation from doing. You merely relax, ignoring the signal and let its summons go by unheeded. There are a great many bells or stimuli in our environment which we continue to respond to from habit, whether or not the response makes any sense. Many people learn to fear strangers because they were told as a child to, "never get into a car with a stranger" or "never take sweets from a stranger." That learned response of fear may serve a useful purpose in childhood but many an adult feels uncomfortable in the presence of strangers simply because of the learned response.

Another person may respond to crowds, closed spaces or open spaces, people in authority-the boss, by feelings of fear or anxiety. The boss, the crowds etc act as "bells" which say danger is present, run away, feel afraid. And out of habit we continue to respond, we obey the bell.

To get rid of the habit of responding automatically to a stimulus we should relax instead of responding.

We can learn to ignore the "bell" as we did with the telephone and continue to sit quietly and let it "ring". A key thought to have in our minds to use whenever we are confronted by any disturbing stimulus is to say to ourselves, "The telephone is ringing but I do not have to answer it. I can just let it ring." This thought will "key in" to your mental picture of yourself sitting quietly relaxed, unresponding, doing nothing, letting the phone ring unheeded, and will act as a trigger or cue to call up the same attitude that you had when letting the phone ring.

When you first try to "uncondition" yourself in this way it may seem difficult to totally ignore the "bell" especially if it rings unexpectedly. Then you can have the same result by DELAYING THE RESPONSE.

I won't worry about that now, I will worry about that tomorrow!

Delaying the response breaks up, and interferes with the automatic workings of conditioning. "Counting to ten" when you are tempted to become angry is based on the same principle, and is very good advice—if you count slowly, and in fact actually delay the response, rather than merely holding in your angry shouting or desk pounding. The "response" in anger consists of more than shouting or desk pounding. The tension in your muscles is a response. You cannot "feel" the emotion of anger or fear if your muscles remain perfectly relaxed. So, if you can delay "feeling angry" for ten seconds, delay responding at all, you can extinguish the automatic reflex.

For example. If you have a fear of crowds and you find

yourself in one and the fear rises and you immediately feel you have to run away, DELAY YOUR RESPONSE by saying to yourself, "Very well, but not this very minute. I can delay leaving the room for two minutes. I can refuse to obey for only two minutes."

We must be very clear in our mind about the fact that our disturbed feelings—our anger, hostility, fear, anxiety, insecurity are caused by OUR OWN RESPONSES—not by externals.

Lack of response means relaxation. You cannot feel unsafe as long as your muscles remain perfectly relaxed.

Tension in muscles is a "preparation for action" or a "getting ready to respond". Relaxation of muscles brings about "mental relaxation" or a "peaceful relaxed attitude". So relaxation is nature's own tranquiliser, which errects a psychic screen or umbrella between you and the disturbing stimulus.

Relaxation means no response and it should be practised daily.

It is important to understand that failure feelings—fear, anxiety, lack of confidence, are attitudes of mind within you and are not caused by anything external. They simply mean that you are underestimating your abilities and overestimating and exaggerating the difficulty before you. You are reactivating memories of past failures instead of past successes.

Feelings cannot be directly controlled by will power. They cannot be turned on and off like a tap. They can however be controlled indirectly. A bad feeling is not dispelled by conscious effort but it can be dispelled by another feeling.

It is the law of substitution.

Remember, that a feeling follows a thought or mental image. So we must immediately concentrate upon a good, positive, desirable image which will counteract the negative image. If we do this the negative feelings take care of themselves.

The only cure for worry is to make a habit out of immediately substituting pleasant, wholesome mental images for unpleasant, worry images.

The past explains how you got here, but where you go from here is your responsibility

The choice is yours. You can keep on playing the "old tape" of the past; reliving past injustices; pitying yourself for past mistakes; all of which reactivates failure patterns and failure feelings which colour your present and your future.

Or, if you choose, you can put on a 'new tape' and reactivate success patterns and "that winning feeling" which help you to do better now and promise a more enjoyable future.

When your cassette player is playing music you don't like, you do not try to force it to do better. You do not use effort or will power. You do not bang the player around. You do not try to change the music itself. You merely change the tape being played and the music takes care of itself. Use the same technique that comes out of your own internal machine. Change the tape. Change the mental imagery and the feelings take care of themselves.

QUESTIONS.

1. Why is it important to forget the past?
2. What is success?
3. What is the difference between remorse and guilt?
4. How can you be a better judge?
5. What is the right way to think of mistakes?
6. What is the first thing to do in dealing with bad habits?
7. Why must we be willing to be a little vulnerable?
8. How do we rid ourselves of the habit of responding automatically?
9. If it is difficult to ignore the "bell" what alternative have you?
10. Is counting to ten useful? How?
11. Why is relaxation important?

SUNSPOTS

**THE LADDER OF
SUCCESS IS NEVER
CROWDED AT THE TOP!**

KEY 10. FORGIVENESS.

SECTION 1. SPRING CLEANING.

In late February or early March we begin to feel the stirrings of Spring. Birds seem active; flowers and early blossom appear; we begin to look ahead to sunny days and holidays.

With the first sharp rays of sunshine on our windows we see the dust and grime left by the wind and rain and immediately feel the need to clean the windows. We do not stop with the windows however. Curtains are washed, carpets cleaned, cupboards and spare rooms are investigated and cleaned up, in fact once a woman starts Spring cleaning the house is usually turned upside down for days and the family heave a sigh of relief when things get back to normal.

This is the time when decorating is done and new furniture bought or cleaned and changed around.

Periodically we need an inner Spring clean.

Our mind is full of old junk, garbage left there years ago. Unless we make an effort now to clean up our attic, our mind, we shall never be as healthy as we wish, as prosperous and fulfilled as we desire to be. We are severely handicapped by the junk of past fears and resentments, hates, worries and anxieties, which clog up the free-flowing energy within us.

Anything that is of no use to us at the present moment should be rooted out and discarded ruthlessly otherwise a state of stagnation and inertia will result.

We have to clean out our attic!

Every problem whatever its nature health, money, work, people, is but a lesson to be learned in the school of life.

We are here to learn, grow and unfold physically, mentally and spiritually.

All experiences, whether we call them good or evil, do not begin somewhere outside of ourselves. They begin within our own mind; our own secret thoughts and feelings.

We have a choice in everything. If we choose to think fear thoughts or any other negative thought pattern we make them firm in our own mind with constant repetition and eventually they become a reality in our life. We then moan and say, "But I didn't ask for this", or, "I have never thought I would have an accident or develop this awful disease".

Our thoughts are cumulative. We constantly give them an airing which makes them stronger in our SCM. They can fester away for years without us being aware of it and eventually come forth in a concrete form.

So, a regular Spring cleaning is necessary.

We are going to cleanse or purify our mind. Do not be put off by the word purify, it is a wonderful healing process which will create riches in your life.

Life is a constant process of purification. We are constantly meeting problems and solving them, But there is more to it than that. We have to learn a lesson from each problem and get rid of all the negative feelings about it, otherwise we shall keep on meeting similar problems until we have finally cleaned out the attic.

It is not enough to pray to God to remove evil appearances from your life. You must find out why they are there and what lesson you are to learn. So where do we start?

The first thing we do is to turn on the light in our attic. This means that we face up to what the problem is, to the fear behind it. There is always fear behind a problem and this has to be brought out and recognised.

We do this by using the power of denial.

We deny that the problem has any power over us, we simply say "no" to it. This will give you a sense of detachment about it, an indifference to it. As you continue to deny that the problem has any power over you, your fear of the situation will leave you.

Please note carefully.

You do not deny that there is a problem. You deny that it has any power over you to upset you in any way.

To keep thinking about the problem and speaking about it is emphasising the problem. That way you are making the problem very firm in your mind and once the SCM gets hold of it then it will be magnified out of all proportion with disastrous results.

The problem is there but you do not accept it in your life by saying an affirmation such as:

This problem has no power over me. It is simply a shadow of my mind caused by my own wrong thinking. I refuse to accept it. There is only good in my life now.

You will feel a new freedom as the "no" power cuts through all the negativity which caused your problem in the first place.

When you say "no" to those situations which upset you, not only will you clear up emotional blocks but you open up a way for the intelligence within you to operate freely and produce a solution.

A member of one of our classes an eighty six year old lady said that she used the "no" power twenty years ago when she was crippled with arthritis. Her affirmation was, "No, I will not accept this diagnosis as permanent. I shall be healed with Divine Intelligence." She worked with this and the other suggestions for six months and the pain disappeared and she has never had a twinge since.

If you say "no" to limiting conditions and remove the fear from your mind about it, you are cleansing your mind and that is the first step on the road to recovery.

The Chinese proverb says that the journey of a thousand miles begins with the first step. Maybe this first step is the one you have to take to begin the complete transformation of your life.

All bad conditions are built up by someone feeling bad about them and this bad feeling not only builds them up but it feeds them. If we remove the bad feeling then we are pulling the rug from under the condition and it then simply fades away.

Bad conditions have no life or substance or intelligence of themselves. They are created by the fears, resentments and other negative beliefs of human beings. We create our own bogeymen. If you refuse to give them any attention by saying as soon as your fear starts, "No, I do not accept this appearance. My life (wealth, health, happiness) cannot be limited. This to will pass and dissolve into its native nothingness." You are cleansing your mind ready for great things to happen for you.

KEY 10. FORGIVENESS.

SECTION 2. RELEASE IT!

The second part of our cleansing or Spring cleaning is renunciation or release, particularly when it comes to human relationships.

Most of the problems in human relationships are caused by trying to get people to do what you think is best for them. You carry this burden around with you and your possessiveness sets up a block in your consciousness so that you are unaware of the inner guidance and illumination you need at this time.

So release means cleaning out your mind of possessiveness. You must cleanse yourself of possessively clinging to the people in your life; telling them what to do in the name of 'love'.

Possessive emotional ties cause you to direct your thoughts and feelings into someone else's life, instead of into your own. You are so busy worrying about others, that all your energy goes into that worry and as a result you deplete your own system.

Release will free you from the awful burden of always trying to dominate or force someone to do your will for their 'own good'. The power of release is wonderful because it frees you of the heavy burden, and it frees the possessed person to grow and unfold in the way that is right for them. So instead of clutching people tightly to you, release them and yourself by saying;

I release you and let you go. I trust the Infinite power within you to guide you and direct you to your highest good.

Whenever that person or that situation tries to get your attention keep releasing by affirming;

I have released you lovingly to the Infinite Intelligence within you and you go to your highest good. And so it is!

Emerson wrote: "If you put a chain around the neck of a slave, the other end fastens itself around your own".

Behind every problem is fear. Behind the problem of possessiveness is the fear of losing a loved one. What we tend to forget or perhaps we didn't know, is that nothing we relinquish is ever lost. Everything finds its true balance, its equilibrium when freed to do so. Each person must have the freedom to grow and unfold naturally in their own way and in their own time, no matter what we feel about it. The way we do things is right, for us. Our way is not right for someone else. We are separate individuals in the school of life and we must unfold and grow in our own time and in our own way without interference.

As you release, you give people freedom in your thoughts about them, to live their own lives, and you are opening up the way for their growth which comes through all their life experiences. They will automatically do whatever is best for themselves at their present level of understanding.

My Grandmother used to say frequently to my Mother whenever we were naughty, "You can't put an old head on young shoulders."

We must all learn life's lessons for ourselves. We cannot grow for someone else, nor can we overcome obstacles for another.

As you release people to their own indwelling Intelligence, you free them to work on the inner pattern or blueprint which is special for them. You have then freed yourself to become open and receptive to your own Intelligence within and so follow the guidance which allows you to follow your own particular path. Let go of the strain; of the pushing and pulling of self-assertion; of the determination to have your own way regardless; stop fighting and struggling mentally.

Relax, release and let go, leaving everything to the perfect outworking of Divine Order.

When you have done all you can in any situation do not keep on trying to force things to happen. That is the time to let go. You then give up your human efforts and accept what comes. You will be amazed at what comes. You will find that the very thing you were striving to achieve will come into manifestation quietly and easily. This is the time for trust and patience.

We have to learn to trust the Infinite Wisdom which is within us all. By letting go and quietly trusting this Inner power to work for us astonishing things result.

Confession is good for the soul.

The Confessions of St. Augustine has been a best seller since 400 A.D. Augustine proved that true peace of soul is found, not so much on the psychological couch, as on the bended knee. That help comes as soon as man realises he cannot lift himself up by his own bootstraps, and then confesses his need to God.

Confession is another healthy form of release. It is the act of confessing to a priest, minister, or a trusted friend. It is an established fact that people who go regularly to a church confessional rarely end up on the psychologists or therapists couch, or in a mental hospital. Confession is a very potent form of release from life's problems. More people are healed through prayer and spiritual treatment than any other methods of healing. We do not always hear of these healings because people keep quiet about them. An ancient teaching says that sacred means secret and by keeping things secret you do not dissipate the energy, nor do you have to face the negative responses of other people regarding spiritual healing.

If you cannot bring yourself to confess to another person then try the spiritual way.

This means going directly to God, or Divine Source. It doesn't matter how you see God. Simply know that deep within you is the Creative Life Force of the universe, the Source of all.

Talk to this inner Intelligence within you, confess to It as you would confess to a priest. Give up the problem to this Source. Do not condemn yourself, you did the best you knew at your level of understanding then. Say, "I give this to you (God), or whatever name you have for the source, for you know what is best for me in this situation."

Another way of confessing is to write it down. Write it all

down in the form of a letter to the Source. Write down everything, leave nothing out. Be perfectly honest about everything, Then place your hands on your written confession and ask God's help and forgiveness. Then give thanks for the cleansing of those mistakes.

The forgiving love of God now frees me from all mistakes of the past and present. I face the future wise, free and unafraid.

This will free you from all guilt and condemnation of yourself.

You should then destroy your written confession and celebrate your freedom.

KEY 10. FORGIVENESS.

SECTION 3. FORGIVE US...

Forgiveness is the third part of the cleansing process. One of the major causes of unanswered prayer is unforgiveness.

You cannot expect good results in your life if you are bound by grudges, prejudices, bitterness and an unforgiving attitude towards God, your neighbour, yourself or the world in general.

Forgiveness can dissolve whatever has stood between you and your good as it cleanses your mind, body and relationships. It will open the way for your dreams to come true.

You can solve more problems through forgiveness than any other way. Whatever your problem is, health, financial or personal relationships they will all quickly respond to forgiveness.

Forgiveness dissolves the emotional blocks and clears up the problem regardless of what other people are saying or doing.

Forgiveness means to "give up" and it is very potent.

The medical profession estimate that 70% of all disease is caused by suppressed emotion. Forgiveness releases that suppressed emotion.

Many people are afraid of the word "forgive". They think it means that they have to do something unpleasant and dramatic. The word simply means to 'give for' to let go of old ideas, feelings or conditions, and to give something better in their place. The "giving for" process forms a vacuum and makes way for new good to rush in. Remember, nature abhors a vacuum.

If you form a vacuum in your mind by practising forgiveness then the good you want in your life will rush in to fill it. Who do we need to forgive?

We need to forgive everyone who has caused us pain and suffering, whether in the past or at the present time. Our loved ones, business or work colleagues, friends, neighbours, anyone who has criticised us or made us feel uncomfortable in any way. Someone may have hurt us physically, or financially, or belittled us in company.

As we go from day to day we sometimes have experiences which can irritate us. We say "good morning" to a neighbour or workmate and they don't respond. The checkout queue at the supermarket is long and the person before you fumbles and fusses and asks irrelevant questions which cause unnecessary delay. In one day we have so many small irritations which can build up and become real or imagined grievances.

All grievances, hurts and grudges must be forgiven. If you cannot do this immediately then set aside a short period of time in the evening just before you go to sleep, when you really get down to reviewing the day's events, and forgive every person or situation which has irritated or annoyed you.

It may help if you make a list of all that happened during the day and analyse the irritating or frustrating things to see why they annoyed you. How were you feeling at the time? Were you cheerful and happy or were you feeling a bit below par? Had an old grievance reared its ugly head?

Do be aware that your own thoughts at the time of the annoyance are very important. What you are thinking and feeling colour, your attitude to everything that you see and hear. Also be aware that other people have their own problems and their own attitudes cause them to do and say things that, in their better moments, would never happen.

Having dealt with the daily forgiveness list you now have to deal with the past and this is more difficult than the present.

The past is made up of memories that are good and bad. We tend to use our energy on the past hurts which have long since gone. As we said previously, old memories are just memories they should not be emotionalised or remembered. Many people say they can forgive but they cannot forget. Well, if you have forgiven then automatically you will forget and be free from the past.

Dig out these old hurts for the last time. Make a list and analyse them. What part did you play in that happening?

You did something which caused that to happen and this needs a lot of soul-searching and honesty to bring it out. Nothing happens by chance, it is cause and effect. As you inspect past events they should now be looked at with more understanding and less blame-laying. We all make mistakes remember and we have to learn from those mistakes and so do other people.

Old wounds really do need rooting out for they are poisoning your whole system. These grievances do not hurt the people who caused them. They cannot. The thoughts you have about them can only hurt you as you are the only thinker in your world and as your thoughts fester away in the deeper parts of your mind over the years, these magnified hurts become malignant growths, ulcers, heart attacks and even early death.

Forgiveness is very important here as you are diffusing a time-bomb which is ticking away inside you! To forgive means to 'let go of' some person, situation or problem. It means we release the particular thing that is bothering us by forgiving it and ourselves. If we are annoyed by something or what some person has done then we must forgive ourselves for being annoyed by it as well as forgiving the person who annoyed us.

Self-forgiveness is an important part of the cleansing process and should be done regularly every night before we retire to bed. Then we give thanks for the release this will bring.

As you work at this you are forming a vacuum in your mind. Scientifically, nature abhors a vacuum and rushes in to fill it with substance. When you form a vacuum in your mind then you must fill it by affirming and visualising the things you want in your life now. If this is not done then negative thoughts will quickly rush in and fill the vacuum.

So, always say affirmations after you have denied and forgiven, then things will start to move in a healthy direction and the good you seek will manifest in your mind, body and affairs.

A FORGIVENESS TECHNIQUE.

Sit for half an hour every day and mentally forgive anyone you are out of harmony with, or feel badly about, or you are concerned about. If you have accused anyone of injustice, if you have discussed anyone unkindly, if you have criticised or gossiped about anyone, if you are legally involved with anyone, mentally ask their forgiveness. Subconsciously they will respond. If you have accused yourself of failure or mistakes, forgive yourself. Forgiveness will form the vacuum that will unlock the floodgates of your prosperity, health and success.

I forgive myself and others. All is well between us. Divine love and Divine justice takes care of everything now. Thank you.

KEY 10. FORGIVENESS.

SECTION 4. HAPPINESS HEALS!

If you want to be happy make someone else happy.

We control our own health by our attitudes towards ourselves and others. This fact was well known by all the philosophers throughout history.

Plato said, "If the head and the body are to be well, you must begin by curing the soul (SCM)."

Solomon said, "A cheerful heart causeth good healing. But. a broken spirit drieth up the bones."

A spirit that is subjected to depressed conditions, that is broken and discouraged usually gets a physical reaction. A baby I know was born into a home where there was severe discord between the parents. The child cried incessantly, was quiet only when picked up and cuddled. As he grew older he developed hearing problems. He had severe inflammation of the ears, earache and deafness. Various treatments failed. Finally he saw a specialist who told the mother there was no physical reason for the trouble, his ears were perfect. I advised the mother that the boy was shutting out psychologically what he could not bear to hear, the many nasty and violent scenes he saw and heard between his parents. I suggested working on forgiveness and sending thoughts of love to each situation no matter how bad it may seem. Also to stop criticising her husband and forgiving him instead. The child is now totally free from his ear problems.

Throughout the lessons we have emphasised the importance of dwelling on the good, positive things instead of on the negative, awful things that happen to us. If we wish to be healthy, happy, prosperous and highly successful, it is vitally necessary to make peace with those we are feeling resentful towards. Unless we do this all our efforts for achieving success will be to no avail. Forgiveness is the foundation of healing. If your finances are out of order they need healing. If your personal relationships are out of order they need healing. If your body and affairs are out of order they need healing. Forgiveness in all these situations will bring about healing. Physical, mental, emotional and spiritual healing is brought about by forgiving ourselves and others each day.

Learn to look at your problems dispassionately. Do not analyse them from a psychosomatic viewpoint, trying to probe into the mental, emotional reasons for the health, financial, or personal relationship challenges in your life.

Use an affirmation such as:

I fully and freely forgive everyone past or present who need forgiveness from me. I let go all resentment and substitute love. The Universal Intellegence is guiding me to peace, prosperity, health and happiness, I give thanks that it is so.

If your attitudes and emotions are constructive and positive you are three quarters of the way there towards perfect peace, abundance, the right work, the right relationships and complete fulfillment.

Make no mistake. To forgive does not mean that you have to bow and scrape to those you feel have wronged you. You do not meed to make any outer contact with those people, unless something crops up that is unavoidable.

They will feel your mental and emotional forgiveness and they will release any animosity they hold towards you.

As you mentally and emotionally let go, of people and situations that are challenging you, by daily affirmations of forgiveness you will experience a new sense of release, as if a great weight has dropped from your shoulders. Most people carry the weight of the world on their shoulders. They carry a heavy burden of their own making. I have seen students straighten up and look inches taller after working with the principle of forgiveness. They lost the stoop, the rigid set of the shoulders and they said how light they felt as though a burden had been taken from their shoulders.

A note here. As you forgive the irritations of people, also immediately forgive yourself for being irritated by them! This is important.

When you start forgiving you may begin to remember things that happened years ago which you had forgotten, but your SCM never forgets. As you work consistently on forgiving, you are disturbing a lot of garbage still in your SCM which will now come to your surface mind, your CM, for you to work on.

Look upon this as part of the cleansing process and regard it as success. It is the mind barrier we talked about earlier. All you now have to do is to face up to whatever comes up and realise it was in the past, you learned a great deal from it, and now you give thanks for the cleansing from it and know with absolute certainty that it will rest in peace. Many students keep a note book and write down these things that come up from the SCM under the heading of R.I.P. This was originally suggested by a student who had a lot of stuff coming up and he found it worked. Whenever things came up, he dealt with them and then wrote them in his R,I,P, book. He put them to sleep for good when he entered them in the rest in peace book.

You will always know if you really have forgiven. Whenever a person or event is brought to mind and you no longer feel disturbed by it, or there are no feelings at all about it, then you have really let it go. If there is any slight feeling left then you haven't quite forgiven, so keep on working at this until it goes right out of your mind.

"FORGIVE SEVENTY TIMES SEVEN"—
JESUS CHRIST

Now, let's get back to the vacuum idea. This can work practically in every aspect of your life, for instance;

As a public speaker I need a constant change of clothes. So whenever I feel I need new clothes I form a vacuum by looking through my wardrobe and taking out clothes that I no longer wear. These are always good clothes but I like to stimulate interest by not wearing things too often at one place. I take them to the local charity shop or give them away to people. I let them go. Now this is very important. I let them go before I think of getting new clothes. Then, I think about the kind of clothes I want and make a list. Sometimes when I have need of clothes for a special occasion I cut out pictures of the kind of clothes I want. I then frequently look at this visual aid and make affirmations. When this is firmly fixed in my mind I then leave it. I let it go and know with absolute certainty I will get exactly what I need.

It never ceases to amaze me how these clothes come. I can suddenly get an urge to go to a certain store whilst out shopping and sure enough I see the exact thing I want. And what is stranger still, I always have enough money on me to pay for it. I must add that I do not set out with the idea of buying clothes, in fact, I never think about clothes. I just let it go. Even when I have no money to buy new clothes I frequently have new clothes given to me as presents, either new clothes or material to be made up. My elder daughter, as a hobby, designs and makes clothes, so she will make up original things for me to wear.

It seems as though I am endlessly giving clothes away and getting new ones without any effort on my part.

If you need to lose weight then maybe you have to let something go? If you hold on to things and people, past or present, then you hold on to everything else in your life, including unwanted weight. I taught many classes to "THINK SLIM" and results came easily when we worked at forming a vacuum and forgiveness.

Everything starts in the mind. If you want health, wealth, success, good relationships, perfect work or business, then you must think, speak and act as though you already have it.

To be healthy means you will be happy. Healthy does not just apply to your body and mind, but also to your money, to your work, to your relationships, in fact everything in your life.

Healthy thinking produces a healthy mind and body. It also produces healthy circumstances in your life. If every aspect of your life is in order then you will be healthy and you will be happy, very happy indeed!

QUESTIONS.

1. Why must we make an effort to clean out our attic, our mind?

2. What should we learn from our problems?

3. What is the power of denial?

4. What causes the most problems in human relationships?

5. What does release mean?

6. How can confession help in releasing?

7. What can forgiveness do for you?

8. Who do we need to forgive?

9. Why do old wounds need rooting out?

10. What controls our health?

11. Do you have to "bow and scrape" to forgive?

12. What happens when you form a vacuum?

SUNSPOTS

**I WILL NOT LET MY
GRIEVOUS PAST WITH
VAIN REGRETS
TORMENT ME—I CAN't
HELP FEELING THAT
MY ACTS DON'T REALLY
REPRESENT ME.**

Rebecca NcCann

KEY 11. AND THE GREATEST OF THESE...

SECTION 1. THE GREATEST SECRET.

I have a secret!
> Do you want long life?
> Do you want perfect health?
> Do you want to look younger?
> Do you want wealth and prosperity?
> Do you want to overcome sickness easily or never to be ill?
> Do you want a better posture and blood circulation?
> Do you want better relationships?
> Well you can have all these things and more.
> How?

Love is the answer.

Love has been called the physician of the universe, the medicine that heals all disease.

Why?

Love is more than an emotion or a spiritual power; it is also a mind power. Because it is a mind power it affects every aspect of your life.

Your mind is operated by thinking and if you think loving thoughts there is a corresponding chemical change in the body cells which is not only beneficial it is life-giving.

By mentally concentrating upon love a very positive love-current will be produced which circulates around the body to break up and dissolve any negative thoughts of hate and resentment.

The resentful thoughts will be dissolved in your mind and also in the mind of the one you are resenting. Such is the power of love.

Suppressed emotion is the cause of 70% of all disease. Regret, remorse and sorrow tear down the body structure. Hateful thoughts generate a deadly mental poison which will eventually destroy the body if it is not neutralised by thoughts of love. In fact all disease comes from the violation of the law of love.

The mind power of love is located behind the heart. It is a ganglionic nerve centre. There is a close connection between this centre and the heart itself.

We feel our emotions in this area and the saying, "she died of a broken heart", is not far wrong when you think of the damage done to that sensitive area by thoughts of rejection and the feeling of being unloved.

Any time we violate the law of love by expressing thoughts and words of fear, hate, resentment and other unhealthy emotions we affect the heart lung area.

The tissue in this area is very fine and is easily affected by negative emotions. Heart trouble and cancer of the heart and lungs results from suppressed emotions, frustration in love and a general feeling of being unloved or repressed by love.

Psychologists tell us that the fear and domination of a mother over her child can be mainly responsible for the diseases and accidents the child suffers.

Many years ago people thought and openly expressed the thought, that if a woman did not worry about her child she was a bad mother. When parents worry about their child and are fearful and anxious for it they are communicating the fears and anxieties to the child. The child subconsciously responds to the negative vibrations produced by their fears and worry.

The SCM of the child is ultra sensitive to the feelings and emotions of the parents so worry and fear are easily communicated and this results in a feeling of limitation, suppression and inadequacy in the child which expresses itself as behaviour and health problems in both the child and the parents, particularly the dominant parent.

As Head Teacher in a Secondary school I had to frequently deal with the results of many oppressed children. Some were rejected, some were suffocated with love. Some parents feel they have a right to dominate the child's life. The child or children, were made to feel guilty if they did not conform to the parents will.

"I know what is good for you." This really means, "You are going to do what I want whether you like it or not, because I say so."

Parents become very aggressive when confronted with the wrongdoing of their child. There is usually a long tirade about how good they are to the child and the child shrivels and is too afraid to speak the truth of the situation.

The poet Elizabeth Barrett was an ailing child and woman under the dominating will of her father. When she found love with Robert Browning she left the ruthless father and started a new life of radiant health and real love.

Our children are not our possessions. They are separate souls with their own identity. Parents are the physical means by which they come into the world and usually they are begotten out of a love relationship.

They need guidance, love and support from parents as they grow and develop and realise their own potential. There should be no following in fathers footsteps or mothers as the case may be.

They have their own talents and latent abilities within their own SCM and if these are not realised and expressed fully the result is a delinquent child and an apathetic adult in later years.

A child is guided by love from parents. If a child is loved he will be loving. If a child is hated he will learn to hate. Parents can actually smother a child with love, at least what they think is love, so that they literally drive the child's soul out of the body and death follows.

This also happens in adults. If one partner is possessive the one possessed will eventually develop heart trouble, become chronically ill and die before his or her time. The one who is left feels cheated somehow, because, "I gave all my love."

Love is a harmonising, balancing, freeing quality of mind and body. It does not bind, possess or dominate, neither is it wilful.

Words of love have a balancing effect on the body. So if you are surrounded by criticism and ill will of any kind, you can retain your sanity and equilibrium by refusing to answer back or get involved in any way. Simply affirm silently to yourself, **"None of these things move me, for UNIVERSAL Love is at work. This too will pass."**

And if other people are in a similar situation you can silently say for them, "UNIVERSAL Love is at work protecting you. None of this moves you, you are surrounded by UNIVERSAL Love and all is well."

Affirmations like this will neutralise all criticism and hostility.

As you meditate on UNIVERSAL Love it comes alive in the heart lung area and will flow through your entire body cleansing, harmonising and purifying it. This will affect your emotions by bringing love and peace of mind. You will understand your relationships more fully and they will be more harmonious. You will become a magnet attracting all kinds of good to yourself and your world will change for the better.

KEY 11. AND THE GREATEST OF THESE...

SECTION 2. I LOVE ME!

At the beginning of the course we emphasised the importance of liking ourselves and eventually loving ourselves.

Jesus gave us the first great commandment: "Thou shalt love the Lord thy God with all thy heart, with all thy soul and with all thy mind and with all thy strength."

And the second great commandment:

"Thou shalt love thy neighbour as thyself."

Before you can obey the first commandment, and indeed the second one also, you must be able to love yourself.

Now this is not an ego trip.

Once you understand your relationship to God, man and the universe, you will think in an entirely different way.

If you can hold the image in your mind that the tremendous power within you, the great creative, life force, is the "I AM" of your being, and the personal ego is the little, insignificant "i", then you will understand that, loving yourself, is not loving your ego, but the great "I AM" within you, the Source of all.

It might help you also to think of all the good, positive, constructive things you say and do, as coming from the "I AM"; and the mean, nasty negative, destructive things you say and do, as coming from the ego, the little "i ".

Always try to differentiate between the two "I AM" or "i", when thinking. This is a way of gaining self-control. Say to yourself, "which 'eye' was that?" If you frequently think from the little "i" then change your thinking immediately, so that you are always thinking from the standpoint of the "I AM". You will find that your responses are not as quick or thoughtless as they used to be, and you are becoming much more tolerant towards yourself and others.

It is vitally important to your peace of mind, to your health, to your finances, to your personal relationships, to your job or business, that you love yourself.

What you think about yourself colours your attitude to everything else.

Remember, that what you feel about yourself was formed years ago when you were a child. All the fears, beliefs and prejudices are not your own, but were passed on to you by all the people in your childhood environment.

Now that you know better, you can root out all things that are not beneficial to your welfare at this present moment.

If there is anything that you do not fully understand, then go back to the lessons which can enlighten you. This course is a course for life. Each time you read it you will gain a greater insight from the reading.

Each day will see further growth and enlightenment and you have all the time in the world.

Right now you must feel very good and comfortable about loving yourself. If you have to go over any exercise, then do so with a greater insight.

The mirror technique should still be continued until you are very comfortable and happy with it. I cannot emphasise this enough.

Love is the key to a great future!

Forgive yourself for all past mistakes, you are still in school remember and you will be until you choose to pass through transition to the next dimension. We are here to grow, expand and achieve all our cherished dreams.

Love will open up the way.

We all need love!

We not only need love and appreciation from other people but we need self-love and appreciation.

When Jesus said that we were to love God with all our mind, heart and soul He meant that we were to love the God Presence, or the Good that is within us, as well as a universal God.

So now start to love yourself, love your life and affairs, love your body, look for and love the good in your life right now.

Some people feel guilty about their desire for love in its

many phases. they feel they should suppress that desire, that it is wrong to desire love and express it.

How wrong and misguided they are.

It is now time to realise that you should express your desire for love—from the inside out.

It is natural and right that you express your desire for love. That is what you were created for. Your Creator made you in His own image and likeness and He is Unconditional Love.

You have the Divine Love potential within yourself and this must be expressed if you are to fulfil your own pattern or blueprint.

You start by taking conscious control of your thoughts and feelings.

Take a few moments each day to develop an impersonal consciousness of love. This will not only help you solve your problems but will also help mankind in general. Affirm:

"I am deliberately and joyfully radiating UNIVER-SAL Love to myself, my world and to all mankind."

Repeat this affirmation often. Then form a mental picture of yourself as healthy, prosperous, illumined, harmonised, and unlimited.

Quietly love that mental picture.

Then affirm: **UNIVERSAL Love is now made alive in me.**

As you work with this mental picture, loving it and affirming, think of love as being a radiant light that enfolds you, that brightens, illumines and uplifts you.

Think of love as a pure white light which contains all the colours of the rainbow, that permeates, penetrates and saturates your whole body.

Feel this pure white light of love penetrating into every atom of your being.

If there are any dark areas in your body or your life think of them as coming alive with the light of UNIVERSAL love and being adjusted.

Continue to meditate on UNIVERSAL love within yourself and visualise it as white light going into every part of your body and all your affairs. Say the affirmations and visualise.

Dare to consciously love yourself. Dare to love every part of your body. Dare to love all your affairs and negative situations.

When you 'see' and feel a satisfying reaction to your meditation—of the light of love flooding your whole being, you then know that you have actually released the greatest power on earth into your mind, body and affairs. You will have new energy, power, poise, peace of mind, prosperity, beauty, harmony, in fact new good in every phase of your life.

MEDITATION

Get into a relaxed state as you were instructed previously. Close your eyes.

Now visualise about twelve inches above your head a pure white light.

Make the picture as real as you can. Work on this until you feel you can see this white light just above your head.

Now imagine that this beautiful white light slowly descends touching the top of your head. Feel it there.

When you actually feel this light, it may seem cold, or you may feel a tingle at the top of your head where it touches you. It is a gentle touch and gives you a good feeling.

This white light contains peace and love. Peace and love.

It now slowly covers your head and face and neck. feel the cool, tingling as it goes further down, across your shoulders arms and hands. Your hands tingle when it gets there!

Down it goes through your body, back and front -then across your hips, down your legs, right down to your toes.

You are now covered in the pure white light of peace and love.

Focus your attention on your heart area. Imagine your heart is filled with this pure love light. Affirm:

UNIVERSAL love fills my heart and overflows into every atom of my being and I am healed in mind, body and affairs now! Give thanks and say, IT IS DONE!

KEY 11. AND THE GREATEST OF THESE...

SECTION 3. I LOVE MY NEIGHBOUR.

You are a unique individual.

So is everyone else!

This uniqueness makes each human being very special, very special indeed. No other human being has your special talents and abilities. Only you can give those talents and abilities to your family, your work, your hobby, your friends, your neighbour.

Your contribution is very important in the scheme of things. Because you are special you are needed!

Once you are secure with this, and that security comes from loving yourself and recognising that mistakes are learning experiences, you can then focus on your neighbour.

Who is your neighbour?

Just about everyone you come into contact with during each day.

It doesn't stop there either.

You view the world at large through your TV set and all the other media, newspapers, books, magazines and radio.

We are constantly making choices. We choose to read a newspaper that more or less agrees with our viewpoint. We take sides in religion, politics, entertainment etc.

Our choice depends upon what we believe at any given time.

As we grow and expand we change quite a lot of our beliefs and we look back with horror at some of the dogmatic and dramatic stands we made when young. Now is the time to make a choice about other people.

We can begin by acting as if we really liked other people!

I remember as a child, about eight or nine years old, actively making a choice to like other people. I only had one real friend and I didn't really want anyone else. I was essentially a loner. I took very little notice of my peer group, although I was well liked and even popular when I made them laugh with my humour.

I had seen bullying of smaller children by both girls and boys and I began to dislike the bullies, even though they had never bullied me. This feeling of dislike I had, bothered me. I could not rationalise it then, but I knew that I basically liked people. So one day as I sat on the swing, the thought came to me that I should pretend to like the bullies and everyone else who irritated me, including some teachers!

I pondered on this for days. Then eventually I deliberately began to seek out the bullies and people I didn't care for and I spoke to them with a smile on my face.

It was quite incredible. I don't know who was the most astonished, them or me! I had always felt that these people were not worth knowing if they acted so rudely and nastily to others. I suppose I had just ignored their very existence.

Now, this cold creature, me, was actually speaking to them and also smiling. It quite knocked the stuffing out of them, but they liked it. Eventually, we became friends. I then found that I had friends from everywhere and I liked it.

The astonishing thing was, although I had told myself to pretend to like them, I found that I genuinely did like them.

I liked them but I did not like what they did at times.

We are all at different levels of development and this is the natural order of things. It is our own responsibility to be able to live harmoniously with everyone regardless of these differences. It is essential for our own development and growth that we make the required effort to try to understand other people and their differences.

People hurt inside. Sometimes their lives seem intolerable. They have little hope of things ever changing. They are caught in the firm net of negativity and discouragement and can see no way out.

In fact such people are usually very aggressive and abusive. They are the ones who are most in need of care and encouragement.

These are the people our neighbours, we should love.

Love comes in many guises.

A word of encouragement gives new hope. A smile means they are recognised as a fellow human being. The touch of a hand on a shoulder when words seem inadequate or inappropriate says, "you are not alone". The swift hug or the holding of hands with a loved one brings comfort and confidence.

These are all ways of loving your neighbour.

We are all part of the same Whole. We are all single cells in the body that makes up mankind. If we love ourselves then we can automatically love our neighbour.

Each human being is a mirror image for us. If we hurt, we see hurt in our neighbour. If we love, we see love in our neighbour.

It is our responsibility to love ourselves, to love your neighbour as yourself, if we are to be happy, successful and fulfilled.

Some years ago Harvard scientists worked on a 'love' project. They discovered that you can actually 'bombard' people with love! Not only people though. You can bombard conditions and situations with love and get seemingly miraculous results.

These scientists predicted that "turning on love" could soon become a universal prescription for healing all the ills of the world.

Every human being needs to feel loved, appreciated and important.

That doesn't mean just you! It means everyone you come into contact with also.

I have found throughout my teaching career that the greatest need is kindness. This need can be easily satisfied just by 'being decent' to people.

No matter how you are provoked or insulted, learn to keep calm. Affirm silently, "**UNIVERSAL love is at work in this situation now and all is well**".

It can help to write out statements of love for people who are hostile.

Write out the persons name and an affirmation, **"UNIVERSAL love is doing Its perfect work in this situation now and all is well"**.

Treat people with love and the results will be amazing.

You do not openly express love to all and sundry, that would be most unacceptable. Just mentally do it. They will pick up your vibes and feel much better for having been in your presence.

LOVE THY NEIGHBOUR!

KEY 11. AND THE GREATEST OF THESE...

SECTION 4. GOD IS LOVE.

Love is the essential ingredient of all the religions of the world. We must love or perish as an individual, a nation, a race of men.

Love is the fulfilling of the Law of creation, or our power to create. We cannot successfully use the creative power within us except within the Law of Love. If you obey the Law of love even a wrong desire will not bring you harm, for love will nullify the wrong desire and you will automatically discard it for a right desire.

"Love has a lot of children. Honesty, kindness, courtesy, patience, gratitude, worship, etc."

"Perfect love casts out fear. It is essential that we cast out fear, for as we have said previously, what we fear will become a reality in our life."

"Love builds your faith and keeps it steady. Unless we believe without any doubts, all our work is useless."

"If you are longing for love, then you must start by being loving towards yourself and others."

"The older we get the more we seem to need love."

"No matter what your dream may be you will need the power of love to make it come true. You have to love your dream."

These are points on love which you should meditate upon daily. Choose a new one each day and work on this list for a month. You will be pleasantly surprised at the results.

The main aspect of God is love.

God is not loving, but Love itself.

The Bible deals with the nature of God and as the Scriptures develop, the idea of God becomes clearer and clearer until nearer the end it says, "God is Love, and he that dwelleth in love dwelleth in God, and God in him", and higher than this we cannot go.

Where there is fear, there cannot be love. The best way to

get rid of fear is to realise UNIVERSAL Love. When you love God more than you love your problem, that problem will be solved.

What you dwell on, give your whole attention to, you love. So, if you love God, or think about God, instead of loving your virus, your grievance your sickness, your lack of money, your lack of personal relationships, your lack of a job, you will be healed.

If you could feel a sense of UNIVERSAL Impersonal Love towards everyone, then nobody could ever hurt you.

UNIVERSAL Love never fails. You must however realise that Love must be in your own heart, it cannot operate from outside, if you see what I mean. If you have sufficient UNIVERSAL Love in your heart for everyone, no matter what their race, colour or creed, then just by affirming you could heal others. This of course is the ideal, Perfect Love.

By the time you reached this stage you would, of course, have got rid of all criticism and condemnation of other people or situations. You would, for instance, never want to see someone punished, or think, "It serves them right". This, of course, does not mean that you would condone any wrongdoing. It means that you would condemn the wrong, but not the wrongdoer.

If a baby cries all night and keeps you awake, or if he breaks an object that you are fond of, you do not hate the baby, you regret the act.

I had close contact with the police when I was head-mistress, over the delinquency and criminal acts of some of the young people in school. There was always kindness shown by the group of officers who were delegated to the schools in the area. There was a close connection between the various departments of the Social Services and school and home.

Sometimes, regretably, the offenders were placed in an institution for the sake of society and for their own rehabilitation. And this was the right thing to do.

In this way you do not allow people to take advantage of you, to impose upon you or cheat you, for this simply helps them to be selfish and dishonest. You must protect your rights, but always in a spirit of UNIVERSAL Love.

A dishonest person really needs UNIVERSAL Love!

How do we get a sense of UNIVERSAL Love?

First we think about it. God is Spirit, not a human being with all the human qualities. God is Absolute Love. God as Love cannot punish, destroy, take away or grudge. We do that in our human way. If we forget the hurts and anger etc and just think about God as Love, then the hurt will be removed.

Then we must analyse it. Try making a comparison with human love and see the difference.

Claim it. As you are a 'child of God' as Jesus said, It is your right to have all that God is, which means everything. God within you is the Source of all. Once you have this realisation, this consciousness, you will never again fear anything or anyone and your life will change completely.

And finally express it. We express this UNIVERSAL Love by practising it towards everyone. That really means seeing the good in each person despite their actions, seeing the good in every situation despite the outer appearance. Nothing is ever what it seems to be. You can only judge by the outer appearance because you do not know the whole story. Remember this. **Nothing is ever what it seems.**

If your present situation is not what you would like it to be, then you can be sure it is lacking in UNIVERSAL Love.

It is a Cosmic law that love heals and fear and condemnation destroys. So watch your thoughts, watch your words and watch your deeds. Make sure that only love finds expression in your life.

Scientific prayer is seeing God, or good, where the trouble seems to be. If someone is behaving badly, see God, or the good, in him. If part of your body is damaged or ailing, see God, or the good, where the problem is. If you are short of money, see God, or the good, in your wallet or purse.

Claim UNIVERSAL Love in each situation, repeat affirmations of UNIVERSAL Love until you begin to feel the presence of this Love within you.

Once you feel the presence of UNIVERSAL Love within

yourself then your demonstration will be made. The thing you need will appear in ways you know not of.

Tell no one what you are doing. This dissipates the energy. Even when the thing you longed for appears, tell no one. Let it crystalise.

God is Love and God is the only power.

QUESTIONS.

1. What is the greatest secret?

2. Why is love so important?

3. Where is the mind power of love located?

4. What is 'smother love' and why is it harmful?

5. What is the difference between the 'I am' and the little 'i'?

6. Why is it important that you love yourself?

7. Why should you express your desire for love?

8. Has meditating on UNIVERSAL Love helped you? How?

9. Who is your neighbour?

10. Whose responsibility is it to live harmoniously with others?

11. What are the 'children of love'?

12. How can UNIVERSAL Love solve your problems?

SUNSPOTS

**WHAT IS IMPORTANT TO
YOU IS NOT SO MUCH
THE CIRCUMSTANCES
OF YOUR LIFE AS YOUR
ATTITUDE TOWARD
THEM.**
Ernest C. Wilson

KEY 12. FULFILMENT.

SECTION 1. IT'S ALL UP TO YOU.

You can have it all!

Whatever you want in your life, you can have.

Whatever you want to do, you can do.

Whatever you want to be, you can be.

Wherever you want to go, you can go.

Whatever you desire, you can have.

There is only one thing that can stop you, the limitation you place on yourself.

YOU LIMIT YOURSELF.

If you have worked consistently this far then you will know exactly what I am talking about and you will agree with me.

You do not have a problem except the one that is in your own mind and you put it there.

Everything begins with a thought and every problem begins with a thought. Isn't it wonderful that you can change this? You can change your own thinking. By now you will realise that you cannot just sit back and expect something to happen. You must make something happen. You cannot sit back and expect someone to do something for you. You have to do it. Everything so far that has happened in your life has happened because of what you did or didn't do. You are responsible for your own life.

Whatever you desire most in life you can have if you are determined to get it the right way. A criminal wants some money. He is determined to get it. The right way for him to get it is to steal it, for he is a criminal.

If you want some money how will you get it? You are not a criminal and you would not condone a criminal act.

There are many ways of getting money, how you get it depends solely upon your level of development. Our development begins from the day we are born and continues until we pass through transition. We are here to learn, for life is a school. How we progress depends upon the lessons we learn from each experience.

If we allow ourselves to be discouraged and defeated by negative situations then we delay our own development. If we work through the negative experiences with hope in our heart and a gentle trusting that the universal Life force will direct us to better things, our development will be progressive and higher than most.

It is according to the level of our development that we think, speak and act. 'You cannot make a silk purse from a sow's ear.' Neither can your development be mature and far-seeing if your consciousness or awareness is at a low level.

Our goal must be for self-improvement. We must be the best we can possibly be in every aspect of our life. We must learn to expect the best.

Real education is not something one learns by going to a brick building for a number of years. Education is a life-long thing which never ceases. As long as we live, we learn. Classroom learning is not more important than life-time learning. Our day to day experiences are valuable lessons in the school of life. Life is an intense, exciting adventure, with education taking place naturally and constantly.

We impose limitations upon ourselves. We judge ourselves harshly. If we were made to feel inferior as children then we feel inferior now and this inferiority limits our desire to achieve. The inadequate feelings rise up from our SCM whenever we need to try a new thing or learn something different. So we make these negative feelings stronger by actually believing them and making excuses for ourselves.

You are never too old to do anything. You can learn anything if you desire it enough. You are teachable. To be successful does not mean you must be young and aggressive. We all need to strengthen our confidence levels for we are all on the path of growth and expansion as we continue in the process of educating ourselves in many different ways. We all travel along individual paths and no person is more than another person, nor less than another. We are all necessary in the scheme of things. We each have our own path to travel, our own part to play and no one else can do this for us. We all contribute to the success of the whole process of life.

We each have our own part of life-education to contribute to the betterment of the whole. We all need to understand. Increased understanding is the reason for life education in all of its forms. Once we understand about life and living we can begin to change in a more positive direction.

Three things that promote understanding.

1. Good, well written books will give us facts which satisfy the intellect.

2. Personal contact and involvement with people at many levels gives emotional experience which fosters empathy with each other.

3. Inner guidance, contacting the Higher power within yourself satisfies your soul.

Working with these three things will bring greater understanding and greater confidence in yourself. The more understanding you have about yourself the more you understand other people.. The more understanding you have, the greater confidence you have. All this brings change in your consciousness, your awareness.

We have already discussed fear. Most people fear change because they fear the unknown. They do not know what will happen if they change, so they would rather stay as they are. Another part of it is that they fear what other people will say about them. Recognise that fear is simply a shadow of the mind and has no power only the power we give it by actually fearing it. All the strength you need is right within yourself. It is the peace within the very centre of your being which nothing can disturb. One of the stumbling blocks to success of any kind is the lack of a deep, burning desire.

If you have a burning desire to do something then you will work hard at trying to get it. Let me ask a few questions.

Do you WANT to be happy?

Do you WANT to be prosperous?

Do you WANT to be healed?

Do you WANT fulfilling work?

The emphasis is on the word WANT.

You might say, "Yes, I want more money, but..." By using this one word, but, you are opting out of your responsibility to believe in yourself and also in the great, Creative Life Force of the Universe which is within you.

You are showing that you do not have faith in yourself or in a higher power than yourself. You are virtually saying that you have no power over your own thoughts, words and actions, that you are, in fact, a puppet whose strings are continually pulled this way and that by everyone.

You are saying that you have a very poor opinion of yourself and that you are not worthy of anything better.

What a sorry state of affairs. There are too many people walking around with this defeatist attitude of mind. Their lives are limited and degrading and they die before their time.

Each of us has the power within ourselves to transform our lives. We must learn to listen to the intuitive whisperings of our own heart and then have the courage to 'go for it.'

To clarify your purpose in life ask yourself the following questions:

1. What do I really want out of life?
2. Do I want it enough to do something about it?
3. Can I visualise myself living as I 'want'?
4. Will I recognise it when it comes?

As you meditate upon these questions and wait in the 'silence' you will receive inspiration and answers will come in many forms. Act on the intuitive leadings that you receive, follow each hunch and see where it leads you. Do not be fearful of the unknown. Keep an open mind and heart and be ready to try something new.

There is a certain excitement about trying new things. This excitement gives a sparkle to your eyes, colour to your cheeks, a lightness of step and a hopeful heart.

There is a saying, "If a man is hungry feed him, that will bring warmth, and with warmth there is hope and with hope everything is possible."

Feed your soul with good, positive, healthy thoughts and this will bring the warmth that begets hope and as we have said previously hope is the lifeline which you can grasp and hold onto for a better life.

You deserve the best and you can only get the best if you become the best you can possibly be.

KEY 12. FULFILMENT.

SECTION 2. MY TRUE GUIDANCE.

"Let us labour for an inward stillness, An inward stillness and an inward healing."

Longfellow

There is a very ancient formula for success;

THINK, ACT, WAIT.

Many people think and act, but they do not complete the last
part of the success formula. Why? Well, they have the totally
wrong belief that unless you stay busy all the time there is
something wrong with you. This is quite the opposite of the
truth of your being. It is only if you stay busy all the time that
there is something wrong with you. To be constantly busy,
rushing around doing one thing after another, never allowing
yourself to pause for a moments quiet reflection and rest is the
cause of all the problems that we suffer from.

Trying to rush around and accomplish as much as you
can during the day then living it up at night is the sure way
to illness, financial ruin and early death.

A young executive in his early twenties worked long,
hard hours at his business. His goal was to make money, as
much money as he could before he reached twenty five. He
not only worked hard but he played hard also. He would
party till dawn then be at his desk by nine. He enjoyed himself. Around him young colleagues did the same, but some
could not stand the pace and resorted to drugs. He did not
use drugs or any other stimulus he just pushed himself to
the limit. Then one day he collapsed. He was rushed to
hospital and stayed there for six weeks. The consultant said
he was a very lucky young man. One of his glands had
stopped functioning and he could have died. He did not
work for three months and during that time he assessed
himself and his lifestyle. His physiotherapist taught him
how to relax mentally and physically and he said that
relaxation changed his way of life.

He learned to let go and relax, to sit quietly in silence and wait for the peace from so doing.

Sitting still in 'the silence' can accomplish more in twenty minutes than eight or nine hours of frantically rushing around being busy. The 'silence' is to the soul what food is to the body. The soul needs nourishment just as the body does to function well. The constant rushing about, the incessant talking of this and that, the perpetual activity throws the body off balance and upsets the internal organs. The 'silence' is a healing balm. It allows the soul to recover from the onslaught of negativity that excess activity brings, and send its vital, regenerating influences to the depleted nervous system and the arteries and veins of the body. Our ragged nerves are restored to normal activity as the soul comes into its own again by sitting in the 'silence'.

How do we practice the 'silence'?

1. Stop what you are physically doing, sit down where you can be undisturbed for about ten to fifteen minutes. Make sure that your back is straight and supported by the chair. Separate your feet and put your hands, palms down, on your knees.

2. Now close your eyes. Mentally say to your body, "relax and let go." Expect your body to follow your thoughts. Say this until you feel your body go limp and feel heavy.

3. Now mentally say to yourself, "I am relaxed in mind and body."

4. Subdue all random thoughts by mentally saying, "Peace be still."

5. Turn your attention within to the centre of your being. Dwell on the nature of the Creative Life Force, the Infinite Intelligence within you.

There is only one presence and one power in the universe, God the good omnipotent. This good is within me and all around me now and all is well.

6. Now just be still and listen. Keep relaxed in mind and body and wait in the 'silence', for 'the still small voice'. If nothing seems to happen, or if you catch your

breath, or feel an impression or a sense of peace, then just give thanks for a perfect result and close the session down.

Now go about your daily affairs.

Inspiration does not always come in the 'silence' There may be a sense of well being, of tranquility. Or you may feel that nothing happened. Rest assured something did happen. It is a time of quiet, peaceful, inner renewal. There will be no flashing lights or vivid experiences!

Do this daily and after a period of time you will feel a tremendous difference in your attitude to yourself and to other people.

ASKING FOR GUIDANCE. When we are in meditation we are open and receptive. We can and do receive ideas from our own SCM or from the race consciousness, or even from well-meaning loved ones who are determined we should follow a particular course which they think is good for u.s.

Our SCM contains all our past experiences and it supplies us with the necessary information so we can make decisions. When we ask for guidance it gives us all the relative information based on past experiences and suggests a direction or solution. Sometimes we think this is the Infinite Intelligence speaking to us and we act on it.

Race consciousness is the collective mind of our culture which says we 'should' act in a particular way. These are ideas and concepts that we learn as we are growing up, without ever being aware of them. Very often our likes and dislikes are governed by this and we feel very strongly about certain things.

The belief in the devil is a good example. Millions of people believe in an evil power and we all, at some point in our development, have held such a belief. The belief of so many people energizes and makes real a concept, that we now know, exists only in their minds. It exists because they believe it exists. This type of strong belief held by so many people produces energies that become part of the consciousness of our culture. Thoughts or beliefs coming from the collective consciousness of our society are very often mistaken for guidance.

Our loved ones mean well when they advise us to do certain things for our own good. They often feel so strongly about it that they are projecting thoughts to us about how we should handle a situation. As we love them we are open to receiving their thoughts and ideas. A mother 'knows' when her child is in difficulty. A mother can be sound asleep and yet hear the slightest sound from her child and awakes immediately. I know, I have three children and was often disturbed by this.

In such a way we can experience thought projections from our loved ones. These thoughts and ideas that come to us from our loved ones can also be misinterpreted as coming from Infinite Intelligence.

How can we discern which is Infinite guidance and which is interference from other sources?

We meditate on it. We simply ask in meditation, "Is this from Infinite Intelligence?"

If it is indeed from the Source of all, it will stay with you. If it is from another source then it will disappear immediately.

Make no mistake, we can get some very strong impressions and inspirations from other sources and because we feel them so strongly we immediately think this is the real thing. If you do not ask the question and just follow the lead then things will not work out for your highest good, in fact it could be disastrous.

Whenever I ask the question and the idea remains, things have gone so smoothly and successfully it seemed unbelievable. When I have forgotten to verify my 'hunch' and have followed through on it, I have come a cropper.

It is essential to let go at least once a day, no matter where you are. Make time for a daily energy boost for yourself by going into the 'silence'. You will be amazed at the difference it will make to your life.

You will be cool, calm and collected on every occasion. Things that are happening around you will no longer bother you for you will know exactly what to do, your intuition will tell you. People will be amazed at how you can cope with difficult things. Your affairs will be in order. Your life style will certainly change. You will really know the meaning of happiness and joy.

KEY 12. FULFILMENT.

SECTION 3. BIRDS OF A FEATHER...

We have many friends in the U.S.A. and some in Kansas City. A few years ago when we were on a visit there I was told the story of Walt Disney. It seems Walt had always loved to draw and he wanted to sell his cartoons. Newspaper editors would not touch them, he was even told that he did not have talent. He was desperate, no money and nowhere to live. The Pastor of a church decided to hire him to draw advertising pictures for forthcoming church events. He had no place to live let alone draw, but the church had an old, mouse-infested garage and he was told he could stay there. It was that humble start to his career that gave Walt the inspiration for his first famous screen character, Mickey Mouse.

That story made a tremendous impression on me. When things seem hopeless there is always a way out. Walt did not give up in despair when editors told him he had no talent. He was destitute, no money and nowhere to live. He did not just curl up in self pity and ask, "why me?" He did not give in to the negative thoughts and feelings that must have come and gone in his mind. He hung in there. He believed in himself. He believed in his own talent and knew he could succeed. He kept on trying all kinds of ways to sell his drawings and eventually the opportunity was there. He did not think of what could happen when this work was over. He fixed his attention on his goal, to sell his cartoons and he worked hard at his drawings. He was determined to do the very best he could and from the dirty, mouse ridden garage he drew his inspiration from the pests. That inspiration is still with us after all these years even though Walt is long gone.

It is very easy to give in to negative thoughts and feelings. It takes courage and determination to get out of the negative rut that constant dwelling on the negative brings about.

Like attracts like. Whatever we think and feel will manifest in our lives. That is the law. Remember we are working with law or principle, the law of attraction. Birds of a feather flock together. Thoughts of a kind have a natural affinity and negative thinking will draw back to us negative results. We have attracted them. We cannot blame others for our own thinking can we? On the other hand, if we constantly have good, positive, constructive thoughts, these will attract back to us the same kind of results. Our positive thoughts activate the world around us positively. We send out good vibes and good vibes attract good things to us. We must work and keep on working, think and keep on thinking, believe and keep on believing. We must never let up, never give in to negativity. Then we will attain our goals, our dreams will come true and seeming miracles will happen.

What is a problem? A problem is a set of circumstances for which there seems no solution. There is always a solution and all you have to do is find it. Once you have found the solution there is no more problem. The first thing to do is to start thinking hopefully. You must cut out the dreary thinking because that brings dreary results. There is a solution and you are clever enough to think of it. Never say anything is impossible or a failure. You have the mental capacity to think your way through any problem if you draw upon the wonderful power of your mind. Think positively, constructively, hopefully, get all your mental powers working creatively and things will turn out better than they are now. If you believe and have faith in the power of your own mind this will light up the darkness of the negative situation and you will see a way through.

Negative thoughts are unhealthy and they pollute your body and the atmosphere. Unhealthy thoughts fester away inside you and all your actions are governed by those unhealthy thoughts. The inevitable result is you cannot see the good that is in yourself, that is in other people or in the world. They destroy your enthusiasm, your creative ability, they make you tired, depressed and old before your time. Who wants that?

People who are alive and vital and enthusiastic are the go-getters of this world. They are not content to sit back and wait for something to happen or for someone to do something for them. They think, plan and work at what they love to do.

Whatever it is you want in your life right now you can have. The first thing to do is to get an idea, then develop enthusiasm for it and finally go to work on building it into a reality. You can do it!

In the 1970s I attended a writing course in California from which I learned many things, including how to write a song! I was most impressed by our teacher and the one outstanding thing I learned was to stop criticising what I had written. She called it the 'critic on your shoulder'.

In other words, we all have an imaginary critic sat on our shoulder that will immediately criticise whatever we write. We write a sentence and immediately we criticise it. Instead we should simply get on with the writing and finish it before we allow the critic to go to work.

THINK FIRST CRITICISE LATER! This principle can be applied to most situations not just writing. I get students to take a piece of paper and pencil and then think about their goal or write it down. They must then go within themselves and ask for ideas on the subject. The goal is the drawing power for ideas if you like, it is the decoy duck. I insist that they write down each idea that comes to mind without stopping to think about it. They leave their critic on their shoulder unattended. Ideas must flow without any editing. When they feel they have done enough or their paper is full, they can group the ideas that are in association and as they do this be ready to add other associated ideas. It is amazing how the ideas flow. All this is done without editing or criticism.

By this time they have groups of ideas and they always find that at least three groups can be worked with after criticism and editing. There is group discussion where they discus each others ideas and this helps to consolidate. The successful way to have an idea is to have lots of ideas and if you defer your criticism you will produce lots of good ones. If your self image is low you will not trust your own ideas. You will make all kinds of excuses for not using them. It is not practical, it will cost too much, its been done before, its too obvious, etc.

This happens because you are editing and evaluating each idea as it comes into your CM. Because you do not think very much of yourself you do not trust the ideas that come, so editing them first gives you the excuse you need for not trying them.

When I taught English I gave each student a 'rough' book. In it they wrote out their ideas without correcting their mistakes. I told them to write down everything that came up without thinking about it. They corrected afterwards and rewrote it into their books for marking. This gives confidence as you know the sorting out will be done later. The object of the exercise is to get something down on paper, lots of ideas, which can be worked on later.

Inside you are tremendous talents that are longing to emerge. You have great qualities you can only dream of now. The only way you can realise these things is to relax, let go and let the powerhouse within you go to work.

Ignore the critic on your shoulder which says, "if only". Those are two of the most dangerous words you can use, almost as dangerous as "I can't." "If only" and "I can't" are defeatist words. They lead to a dull, frightened attitude towards things. It is negative and is linked with the past.

If you substitute "next time " for "if only" or "I can't" you are displaying a positive, courageous attack on problems and it will motivate you to do your best and move ahead in a positive way, free from limiting negative feelings.

Do one job at a time and live one day at a time. Remember we are always in the NOW. A successful person lives in the now and is always heading toward next time!

KEY 12. FULFILMENT

SECTION 4. YOU CAN DO IT!

Practically all my life people around me have said, "You can't do that", with the emphasis on the 'can't'. Whatever it was they thought I could not do, I felt just as strongly that I could. I never argue with anyone, I just go quietly ahead and do what I think is right for me to do. As a child this caused problems. I was called defiant, a bad influence, different from other people. The strange thing was that whatever I did against all opposition turned out to be right, but this was never acknowledged by the people who had said, "you can't".

As an adult I learned not to be hurt by this kind of thing and consequently what I did was acknowledged and praised. I was called an innovator. I was the one who had the ideas and worked out a way for those ideas to be used in a practical sense.

This did not happen because I was different from anyone else, it came about because I knew I did not feel happy if I went along with the suggestions or commands of other people, when these commands did not seem right for me to do. I was not defiant. I knew within myself that I could do something and conversely I knew if I couldn't.

If you work consistently with these principles then your life will change. You will be an innovator, the one with the ideas which others cannot come up with.

BE TRUE TO YOURSELF! Your inner urges are very important, they can make the difference between a mediocre existence or a very highly successful life. These inner urges come from the creative power deep within your SCM. The Creative Power of the universe is within you and needs to express in you and through you.

It can only do this if you are ready and willing to let It. We have been so conditioned by parents, grandparents, teachers, our peer group, that we actually fear the unknown. We are afraid to try something new, something different. We feel very safe in our comfortable rut and if things do not turn out as we wish they could, then that's the way it is.

That is not the way it is. That is the fear way. The successful way is to listen to the promptings of your inner self, your conscience, call it what you will. Throughout the centuries there have been people who have done this and as a result we benefit today. Make no mistake about this, we would not be living in a world full of modern comveniences had someone not had the idea to improve on the way things were done. If man had not used his inner power, his imagination we would still be living in the stone age.

Everything starts with an idea in mind. A building is not just put up for the heck of it. An architect has an idea. He mulls it over in his mind. He doodles on paper until the idea takes shape. He then works out precisely the measurements and draws a detailed plan which includes all the materials needed to build. He is clear and precise in his detailed drawing. This, is then passed on to the builder who in cooperation with the architect starts to organise the men who will erect this building. The construction is carefully monitored and supervised and after a time the idea is a beautiful building exact in every detail of the plan. The idea is made manifest.

You are the architect of your own life. Your ideas become your plan or blueprint from which your life is built. Have you planned carefully? What about all the details? Is your life plan as exact as you can get it? You are not only the architect but also the builder of your life. What kind of a construction have you made so far? Is it as beautiful as you would like it to be? Does it have all the things you want in it? Is it in it's right location? Is it strong, healthy, prosperous and free of limitation? You as the architect and builder of your life can change it if it is not to your own satisfaction. You can start again. Isn't that great! You can start again. It is never too late to change.

Be aware of the excuses you will make for not having as good a construction as you would like, the alibi's—the self-deceit. You are never too young, too old, too ignorant, too this or that. These excuses are your fears being allowed to take over and they are your downfall, your destruction.

If there is something you want to do then do it. Go for it! You never know if anything will work until you try it.

A married woman with a husband, three children and a house to look after suddenly got the urge to better herself. She was highly intelligent and an avid reader, but somehow she no longer felt satisfied with her lot. She loved her husband, her children and her house, but this was not enough. One day she saw an advertisement for a correspondence school so she cut out the coupon and filled it in. The puzzling thing was she did not know what course to check There were at least twenty five courses listed. She read through and could find nothing she could relate too. For a while she sat there and then said out loud, "What do I really want to do?" Instantly the reply came into her mind, BE A TEACHER. It was as though someone spoke inside her head. Without any hesitation she wrote on the form TEACHING. She posted the letter and forgot about it.

Three days later the thought hit her, "What have I done? I have never thought of teaching before". She was horrified. She consoled herself by thinking that teaching was not on the list of subjects, she had written below the list, so maybe they will ignore it. She hoped so. Four weeks later there was a knock at the door. An insignificant little man stood there. He was from the correspondence school. They talked and he said the best way for her to teach was to take their courses for GCE English and Mathematics. She signed the agreement to pay the fees by instalments and away he went.

As she prepared the evening meal the enormity of what she had signed hit her. Where would she get the money from? She didn't work. The housekeeping money would not stretch to include that. She mulled this over for a few days. Then quite out of the blue her next door neighbour called and said a friend was in desperate need of someone to clean her house as she had broken her leg.

Did she know of anyone who could help out for six weeks? Yes she did, she would do it. The neighbour was delighted.

So without telling her family she worked and earned some money. It paid for the deposit and the first instalment.

She put her all into cleaning that house, so much so she was asked if she would be permanent. She would. Her fame as a house cleaner spread. The word quickly got around that she was fantastic as a cleaner and honest also. Soon she was working every morning.

Came the school holidays. Now she had to tell the family. It was received very well because things had still been running smoothly and they were amazed when she told them. Her elder daughter said, "I won't tell anybody!"

This continued for a year. Then one day she again felt the inner discontent. What to do now? The idea came to write to the Director of Education. She did that, in fact she poured out her heart to him. Two weeks later she had a reply. 'Enjoyed your letter very much. Our policy does not allow us to employ unqualified staff, but am enclosing a list of all the Independent schools here as their ruling is not as strict.' There were thirty schools on the list, she wrote to them all. Two replied, 'a wonderful letter but we are fully staffed.' So she went on working and studying. Six months later, and quite out of the blue, came a letter from the Headmaster of a Boys Boarding school. 'Interested, come and see me'.

She went. She was given the post of unqualified teacher for the seven to nine year olds, with supervision duties of the prep period for older boys. She couldn't believe it. She spent the summer holiday working out the lessons she had to take and organised her own family for when she started work.

She was a great success. Her supervised lessons were deemed excellent and she was given more responsibility. The salary was poor, £130 pa. But, this was great experience and she learned a lot.

One morning during her rest break she was reading the paper and a small item seemed to stand out at the bottom of the page.

The headline was, MANCHESTER UNIVERSITY'S EXPERIMENT. The tiny, insignificant account said that Manchester University had realised the vast potential being wasted among mature women who were intelligent yet did not have the chance to become professionals. They felt that this vast potential could be used in teaching and The School of Education were experimenting with the training of older women as teachers. The significant thing for the woman was the last line which said, six of the students had no qualifications at all and the results were outstanding.

That was all she needed. She wrote and was accepted for interview and testing. This meant two days at the University being interviewed, writing essays, doing intelligence tests, working on various papers and more interviews.

She was accepted for the following year!

She travelled daily to Manchester. Fortunately her husband and mother worked a rota system for the children and she had slightly longer school holidays than they did. It was very hard work even so and she had to work long hours into the night to keep up with assignments. The only thing that suffered was the house. One Sunday morning trying to have a lie in the children came to join mum and dad as usual in bed. Her son went out and brought back with him a huge pile of something in his hand. "Look what I have found under my bed," his eyes were shining with delight for it was something he had never seen before. They all looked at his hands in amazement. Triumphantly he lifted up his hands. They enclosed a mound of grey fluff!

She felt mortified. The girls went to see if they had any!

There were many setbacks during those training years. She had major surgery, was involved in a minor train crash, her elder daughter had problems. she almost had a nervous breakdown, but finally it was over. She was a qualified teacher. Her first two years she travel daily to Liverpool as assistant teacher in a secondary school. Then she was appointed head of a department in a very good school in her home town. Two years later she applied for and was appointed deputy headmistress on the south coast and finally became headmistress.

All this came about because she followed a hunch. First she felt a discontent with her lot, she wasn't unhappy she just felt that she should be doing other things. Then following all the leads that came her way. She did not hesitate, or doubt, she just tried it out and she followed the intuitive leads that came from her SCM.

This is a long story but it has been told for a purpose. You can if you think you can.

Do not let others tell you differently. You have all the power you need within yourself, it does not matter what other people think or say about it.

Whenever these thoughts came to this woman she told no one, not even her family. She just followed through and gave it all she had. Her enthusiasm kept her going through the many traumas she experienced. She did not give up! Her affirmation was:

I am going to see this through no matter what. I have spent too much time and energy on it so far to give up now. God is giving me the strength. I will see it through.

That has been my affirmation for many years now. For I was the woman who left school at fourteen years of age. Who went from job to job, forever seeking the fulfilment I knew I could have. When I fell in love and married at twenty years of age I thought I had it. When my children were born I thought I had it. Something was driving me on without my realising it. All the experiences whether good or not so good were caused by my own thinking and feeling. I have had many more happy and glorious experiences than not so good ones. All the time I was learning. Life is a school. Now you see why I make this analogy. I allowed my inner self to guide me without fully understanding why. All I knew was I felt better doing it.

I am still very much in the schoolroom of life. Every day brings me new challenges and experiences. I love life and I live it with love and enthusiasm. I can't wait to try something new.

I am here, as you are, for a purpose. I have things to do that no one else can do like me. I have my contribution to make in the scheme of things. I am forever learning and I enjoy it.

I am healthy, wealthy and wise and I go from strength to strength.

I am here to fulfil the purpose of my life. This also includes being of service. Whenever my particular talents are needed there you will find me. Maybe you will see me in your town, or city.

As we help others we help ourselves that is the law of creation.

Bless each and every one of you.

QUESTIONS.

1. What is the only problem you have in life?

2. Why does a low self-image stop you from finding your true place in the scheme of things?

3. What is your heart's desire?

4. Is discontent a bad thing?

5. Why is the 'silence' important?

6. What are the essential ingredients for success?

SUNSPOTS

ACHIEVEMENT IS BUT
ANOTHER MILESTONE
ON THE HIGHWAY OF
PROGRESS. THE END OF
THE JOURNEY LIES
EVER BEYOND.

CONGRATULATIONS!

You've done it! You have completed all the 48 sections of this course.

Do you realise how far you have come and how much you have learned?

In twelve months you have accomplished what it sometimes takes years to achieve.

You have worked so consistently through each lesson and that requires determination and dedication, two of the most important ingredients of success.

You can feel very proud of yourself at this moment.

So congratulate yourself.

Give yourself a reward—something that you would not normally do for yourself.

YOU DESERVE A TREAT! So whatever that means to you, do it!

Now you have completed this course, do not sit back and think you need not do anything else.

You will have changed some of your old attitudes and as a result certain aspects of your life have changed.

You do not stop there.

Life itself is change and that means we are constantly learning, growing and unfolding in every way.

Read the lessons regularly, particularly the ones you are not too sure about, or maybe skipped through quickly. Make sure that you really understand each section. Revision is essential to continued progress.

Time spent revising is time well spent and each time you do this you will have different insights and understand more fully the real implications of the lessons.

Life is an exciting adventure!

You have only just begun!

SUNSPOTS

**You do not have a
problem except the one
that is in your own mind,
and you put it there!**

Myrtle Fillmore.
Co-founder of Unity.

FOR FURTHER READING

Analytical Psychology

Synchronicity

The Undiscovered Self

Memories, Dreams,   C.G.Jung Routledge
Reflections   London

Psychocybernetics   Dr. Maxwell Maltz

                                              Melvin Powers,
                                              Hollywood, CA.

Power through
Constructive Thinking

Alter Your Life   Emmet Fox. Harper and
                                              Row, NY.

The Science of Mind   Ernest Holmes. Dodd
                                              Mead & Co. NY.

The 12 Powers of Man

Atom-Smashing Power   Charles Fillmore. Unity
of Mind   Books, Unity Village, MO,
Prosperity   USA.

The Healing Secrets of the Ages

The Dynamic Laws of   Catherine Ponder. De
Prosperity   Vorss, Marina del Rey, CA.
                                              USA.

Hidden Power for   Dr Frederick Bailes.
Human Problems   Prentice Hall, NJ. USA.

The Emerging Self	Ernest C. Wilson. Unity Books, Unity Village, MO, USA.
The Infinite Way	Joel Goldsmith. De Vorss, Marina del Rey, CA. USA.
Jonathan Livingston Seagull	Richard Bach Pan Books, London.
How to Win Friends and Influence People	Dale Carnegie. Cedar Books, Worlds Work Ltd., Surrey. UK.
The Power of Positive Thinking	Norman Vincent Peale. Cedar Books, Worlds Work Ltd. Surrey, UK.
The Greatest Salesman in the World	Og Mandino. Frederick Fell, NY. USA.
Think and Grow Rich	Napoleon Hill. Melvin Powers. Hollywood, CA. USA.
Success Through a Positive, Mental Attitude	N. Hill & W. Clement Stone. Prentice Hall. NJ. USA.
Within You is the Power	Dr. Joseph Murphy. De Vorss.
Science of Mind in Everyday Living	Dr. Donald Curtis. Unity Church of Dallas, Dallas, Texas. USA.
The Phenomenon of Man	Pierre Teilhard de Chardin. Harper Brothers, NY. USA.
Tertium Organum	P. D. Ouspensky. Alfred A. Knopf, NY. USA.